MW00891586

THIS BOOK BELONGS TO

The Library of

....

....

Thank you for Purchasing my book and taking the time to read it from front to back. I am always grateful when a reader chooses my work and I hope you enjoyed it!

With the vast selection available online, I am touched that you chose to be purchasing my work and take valuable time out of your life to read it. My hope is that you feel you made the right decision.

I very much would like to know what you thought of the book. Please take the time to write an honest and informative review on Amazon.com. Your experience and opinions will be of great benefit to me and those readers looking to make an informed choice.

With much thanks.

©COPYRIGHT2023
ALL RIGHTS RESERVED

The content contained within this book may not be reproduced, duplicated, or transmitted without direct written permission from the author or the publisher. Under no circumstances will any blame or legal responsibility be held against the publisher, or author, for any damages, reparation, or monetary loss due to the information contained within this book. Either directly or indirectly.

Legal Notice:
This book is copyright protected. This book is only for personal use. You cannot amend, distribute, sell, use, quote, or paraphrase any part, or the content within this book, without the consent of the author or publisher.

Disclaimer Notice:
Please note the information contained within this document is for educational and entertainment purposes only. All effort has been executed to present accurate, up-to-date, and reliable, complete information. No warranties of any kind are declared or implied. Readers acknowledge that the author is not engaging in the rendering of legal, financial, medical, or professional advice. The content within this book has been derived from various sources. Please consult a licensed professional before attempting any techniques outlined in this book. By reading this document, the reader agrees that under no circumstances is the author responsible for any losses, direct or indirect, which are incurred as a result of the use of the information contained within this document, including, but not limited to — errors, omissions, or inaccuracies.

Table of Contents

Introduction   28

You will Need   29

The Projects   30

    Misty Copeland   32

    Frida Kahlo   39

    Rita Moreno   50

    Coco Chanel   61

    Josephine Baker   72

    Maya Angelou   80

    Jane Austen   92

    Bruce Lee   99

    Jackie Robinson   107

    Jane Goodall   118

    Malala Yousafzai   125

    Audrey Hepburn   137

    Serena Williams   148

    Muhammad Ali   158

    Gandhi   169

    Prince   180

    Katherine Johnson   191

    Abraham Lincoln   200

    Pablo Picasso   210

    Rosa Parks   217

Techniques   227

SUMMARY

Inspiring Young Minds with Crochet Heroes: Empowering Creativity and Building Character

In today's fast-paced and technology-driven world, it is becoming increasingly important to provide young minds with opportunities to explore their creativity and develop essential life skills. One such avenue that has gained significant popularity in recent years is crochet. This traditional craft not only allows individuals to create beautiful and functional items but also serves as a powerful tool for inspiring and empowering young minds.

Crochet Heroes, a unique initiative aimed at inspiring young minds, has been making waves in the education and crafting communities. By combining the art of crochet with storytelling and character development, Crochet Heroes offers a one-of-a-kind experience that engages children in a meaningful and impactful way.

At the heart of Crochet Heroes is the belief that every child has the potential to be a hero in their own right. Through the process of crocheting, children are encouraged to tap into their imagination and creativity, enabling them to bring their favorite characters to life. Whether it's a superhero, a princess, or an animal, the possibilities are endless. By creating these crochet heroes, children not only develop their fine motor skills but also learn the value of patience, perseverance, and problem-solving.

The benefits of engaging young minds in crochet extend far beyond the development of technical skills. Crochet Heroes provides a platform for children to explore their emotions and express themselves in a safe and nurturing environment. As they crochet their heroes, children are encouraged to reflect on the qualities and values that make a hero, such as bravery, kindness, and empathy. This process fosters character development and helps children understand the importance of these virtues in their own lives.

Furthermore, Crochet Heroes promotes inclusivity and diversity by offering a wide range of character options for children to choose from. By featuring characters from different cultures, backgrounds, and abilities, Crochet Heroes encourages children to embrace and celebrate differences. This not only promotes a sense of belonging but also helps children develop empathy and respect for others.

In addition to the personal growth and character development aspects, Crochet Heroes also provides a platform for social interaction and community building. Through workshops, classes, and online communities, children have the opportunity to connect with like-minded individuals who share their passion for crochet and storytelling. This sense of belonging and camaraderie fosters a supportive and encouraging environment where children can learn from each other, share their creations, and inspire one another.

Connecting Craft with Role Models of Crochet Heroes: Connecting Craft with Role Models of Crochet Heroes is a platform that aims to bring together the world of crochet enthusiasts with their role models and heroes in the craft. This platform serves as a bridge between the aspiring crocheters and the experienced artisans who have made a significant impact in the crochet community.

The input for this platform is the desire of individuals to connect with their crochet heroes. These individuals may be beginners in the craft, looking for inspiration and guidance, or they may be experienced crocheters seeking to learn from the best in the field. Regardless of their skill level, they all share a common passion for crochet and a desire to connect with those who have mastered the art.

The output of this platform is a unique and enriching experience for both the crafters and the role models. For the crafters, they have the opportunity to learn from the best in the field, gaining insights, tips, and tricks that can help them improve their skills and take their craft to the next level. They can also find inspiration in the stories and journeys of their crochet heroes, learning about their struggles, successes, and the lessons they have learned along the way.

For the role models, this platform provides a platform to share their knowledge and expertise with a wider audience. They can inspire and motivate aspiring crocheters, helping them overcome challenges and encouraging them to pursue their passion for crochet. By connecting with their fans and followers, the role models can also build a strong and supportive community, fostering a sense of belonging and camaraderie among crochet enthusiasts.

The platform facilitates this connection through various means. It may include online forums or communities where crafters can interact with their role models, ask questions, and seek advice. It may also include virtual workshops or classes conducted by the role models, where crafters can learn directly from them and receive personalized guidance. Additionally, the platform may feature interviews, articles, or videos showcasing the work and achievements of the role models, providing inspiration and education to the crafters.

Overall, Connecting Craft with Role Models of Crochet Heroes is a platform that brings together the crochet community in a meaningful and impactful way. It allows crafters to connect with their role models, learn from their experiences, and be inspired by their achievements. Through this platform, the craft of crochet is elevated, and a sense of community and support is fostered among crochet enthusiasts worldwide.

The Magic of Amigurumi: Bringing Characters to Life of Crochet Heroes: This book is a captivating and informative book that delves into the world of amigurumi, a Japanese art form that involves creating adorable stuffed toys using crochet techniques. This book is a must-have for crochet enthusiasts and anyone interested in exploring the creative possibilities of amigurumi.

The author, an experienced amigurumi artist, takes readers on a journey through the process of bringing characters to life through crochet. The book begins with an introduction to the art of amigurumi, explaining its origins and the materials and tools needed to get started. The author also provides a brief overview of basic crochet techniques, making this book accessible to both beginners and more advanced crocheters.

One of the highlights of this book is the extensive collection of crochet patterns for creating a wide range of amigurumi characters. From cute animals to beloved cartoon characters, the author provides step-by-step instructions and detailed photographs to guide readers through each project. The patterns are well-written and easy to follow, making it possible for even novice crocheters to successfully complete their own amigurumi creations.

In addition to the patterns, the author also shares valuable tips and tricks for customizing and personalizing amigurumi characters. Readers will learn how to add unique details, such as facial expressions and clothing, to make their creations truly one-of-a-kind. The author also provides guidance on choosing the right yarn and colors to bring out the best in each character.

What sets this book apart from others on the subject is the emphasis on storytelling and character development. The author encourages readers to think beyond the stitches and consider the personality and backstory of each amigurumi character. This adds an extra layer of depth and creativity to the projects, allowing readers to truly bring their characters to life.

The book also includes a section on advanced techniques for those looking to take their amigurumi skills to the next level. From shaping and sculpting to adding intricate details, the author provides clear instructions and helpful tips for achieving professional-looking results. This section is a valuable resource for experienced crocheters looking to expand their repertoire.

Overall, The Magic of Amigurumi: Bringing Characters to Life of Crochet Heroes is a comprehensive and inspiring guide to the art of amigurumi. With its detailed patterns, helpful tips, and emphasis on storytelling,…

Selecting the Right Materials for Your Little Heroes with Crochet: When it comes to creating crochet items for your little heroes, selecting the right materials is crucial. Not only do you want to ensure that the finished product is safe and comfortable for your child, but you also want to choose materials that are durable and easy to work with.

One of the first things to consider when selecting materials for your crochet project is the type of yarn. There are many different types of yarn available, each with its own unique characteristics. For children's items, it is important to choose a yarn that is soft and gentle against their delicate skin. Look for yarns that are labeled as "baby" or "soft" to ensure that they are suitable for your little one.

In addition to the softness of the yarn, you should also consider its durability. Children can be rough on their toys and clothing, so it is important to choose a yarn that can withstand their active play. Look for yarns that are labeled as "washable" or "durable" to ensure that your crochet items can withstand frequent use and washing.

Another important factor to consider when selecting materials for your little heroes is the type of hook you will be using. Crochet hooks come in a variety of sizes and materials, each with its own advantages. For children's items, it is best to choose a hook that is comfortable to hold and easy to maneuver. Many crocheters prefer hooks made of aluminum or plastic, as they are lightweight and easy to work with.

In addition to the yarn and hook, you may also want to consider adding embellishments to your crochet items. Buttons, ribbons, and other decorative elements can add a touch of personality to your little hero's outfit or toy. When choosing embellishments, be sure to consider their safety. Avoid small buttons or beads that could pose a choking hazard, and opt for larger, securely attached embellishments instead.

Lastly, it is important to consider the specific needs and preferences of your little hero. Some children may have sensitivities or allergies to certain materials, so it is important to choose materials that are hypoallergenic and free from any potential irritants. Additionally, consider the colors and patterns that your child may enjoy. Crochet items can be a great way to express your child's interests and personality, so be sure to choose materials that reflect their unique style.

In conclusion, selecting the right materials for your little heroes with crochet is essential for creating safe, comfortable, and durable items.

A Brief History of Hero Archetypes in Storytelling of Crochet: The hero archetype has been a prominent and enduring figure in storytelling throughout history. From ancient myths and legends to modern novels and films, heroes have captivated audiences with their courage, strength, and determination. Interestingly, this archetype has also found its way into the world of crochet, a craft that has its own rich history and tradition.

Crochet, which involves creating fabric by interlocking loops of yarn with a hooked needle, has been practiced for centuries. It has been used to create a wide range of items, from clothing and accessories to home decor and toys. While crochet may seem like a simple and practical craft, it has also become a medium for storytelling and self-expression.

In the world of crochet, hero archetypes can be seen in the form of amigurumi, which are small crocheted dolls or animals. These adorable creations often take on the appearance of beloved characters from books, movies, and video games. They are meticulously crafted with attention to detail, capturing the essence of the hero they represent.

One example of a hero archetype in crochet is the superhero. Crocheted versions of popular superheroes like Batman, Superman, and Wonder Woman have become incredibly popular among crochet enthusiasts. These amigurumi superheroes embody the qualities of bravery, justice, and selflessness that define the hero archetype. They serve as reminders of the power of good and inspire individuals to be their own heroes in their everyday lives.

Another hero archetype that can be found in crochet is the fairytale hero. Characters like Cinderella, Snow White, and Sleeping Beauty have been reimagined as amigurumi dolls, complete with their iconic outfits and accessories. These crocheted fairytale heroes represent resilience, kindness, and the triumph of good over evil. They bring the magic of fairytales to life and remind us of the importance of hope and perseverance.

In addition to superheroes and fairytale heroes, crochet also showcases other hero archetypes such as the warrior, the adventurer, and the protector. These amigurumi creations often draw inspiration from historical figures, mythical creatures, and fantasy worlds. They embody the spirit of adventure, courage, and the willingness to fight for what is right.

The hero archetypes in crochet not only serve as decorative pieces but also as symbols of inspiration and empowerment. They remind us of the timeless appeal of heroes and the universal desire for good to triumph over evil.

Basic Techniques in Amigurumi Crochet of Crochet Heroes: Amigurumi crochet is a popular craft technique that involves creating small stuffed toys or characters using crochet stitches. It has gained a lot of popularity in recent years due to its versatility and the ability to create adorable and unique designs. If you are interested in learning the basic techniques of amigurumi crochet, then you have come to the right place!

One of the first things you need to know about amigurumi crochet is that it requires a specific type of yarn and crochet hook. The yarn used for amigurumi is usually a lightweight, soft, and durable yarn, such as acrylic or cotton. The crochet hook size will depend on the thickness of the yarn you choose, but typically a 2.5mm to 4mm hook is used.

Once you have your materials ready, the next step is to learn the basic crochet stitches. The most commonly used stitches in amigurumi crochet are the single crochet (sc), double crochet (dc), and slip stitch (sl st). These stitches will form the foundation of your amigurumi project.

To start your amigurumi project, you will need to create a magic ring or adjustable ring. This technique allows you to create a tight and seamless starting point for your amigurumi. Once you have made the magic ring, you can start working in rounds or rows, depending on the pattern you are following.

Working in rounds involves continuously crocheting in a spiral, without turning your work. This technique is commonly used for creating the body and head of amigurumi toys. On the other hand, working in rows involves turning your work at the end of each row, similar to traditional crochet. This technique is often used for creating flat pieces, such as arms, legs, and clothing.

As you progress with your amigurumi project, you will also need to learn how to increase and decrease stitches. Increasing stitches allows you to create a wider or rounder shape, while decreasing stitches helps you create a narrower or tapered shape. These techniques are essential for shaping the different parts of your amigurumi toy.

Another important technique in amigurumi crochet is the use of safety eyes and embroidery for adding facial features and details to your amigurumi. Safety eyes are plastic or metal eyes that can be attached securely to your amigurumi, giving it a more professional and finished look.

Understanding Patterns and Symbols of Crochet Heroes: Understanding the patterns and symbols used in crochet is essential for anyone looking to become a crochet hero. Crochet heroes are individuals who have mastered the art of crochet and are able to create intricate and beautiful designs using yarn and a crochet hook. These heroes are able to take a simple ball of yarn and transform it into a work of art.

One of the key aspects of becoming a crochet hero is understanding the various patterns that are used in crochet. Crochet patterns are essentially a set of instructions that guide the crocheter on how to create a specific design. These patterns can range from simple and basic stitches to more complex and intricate designs. By understanding these patterns, crochet heroes are able to create a wide variety of projects, from simple scarves and hats to intricate blankets and garments.

In addition to patterns, crochet heroes also need to understand the symbols that are used in crochet. Crochet symbols are a visual representation of the stitches and techniques used in crochet. These symbols are often used in crochet patterns as a way to save space and make the instructions more concise. By understanding these symbols, crochet heroes are able to read and interpret crochet patterns more easily, allowing them to create their desired designs with precision and accuracy.

Some common crochet symbols include the chain stitch symbol, which is represented by a small "v" shape, and the double crochet symbol, which is represented by a tall vertical line with a horizontal line crossing it near the top. These symbols, along with many others, are used in combination to create various stitches and techniques in crochet.

Understanding patterns and symbols is not only important for following crochet patterns, but it also allows crochet heroes to create their own unique designs. By understanding the underlying structure and techniques used in crochet, these heroes are able to experiment and create their own patterns and designs. This creativity and innovation is what sets crochet heroes apart from the rest, as they are able to push the boundaries of what can be achieved with a crochet hook and some yarn.

In conclusion, understanding the patterns and symbols of crochet is crucial for anyone looking to become a crochet hero. By mastering these elements, crochet heroes are able to create intricate and beautiful designs, read and interpret crochet patterns with ease, and even create their own unique patterns and designs. So, if you're looking to become a crochet hero, start by familiarizing yourself with the patterns and symbols of crochet, and let your creativity and imagination soar.

Tips for Choosing Colors and Textures of Crochet Heroes: When it comes to choosing colors and textures for your crochet heroes, there are several tips and considerations that can help you create stunning and visually appealing pieces. The colors and textures you choose can greatly impact the overall look and feel of your crochet hero, so it's important to choose wisely.

Firstly, consider the theme or concept of your crochet hero. Are you creating a superhero character or a cute animal? The theme will guide your color and texture choices. For example, if you're making a superhero character, bold and vibrant colors like red, blue, and yellow may be more suitable. On the other hand, if you're creating a cute animal, softer and more pastel colors may be more appropriate.

Next, think about the personality or characteristics you want your crochet hero to have. Colors can evoke different emotions and moods, so choose colors that align with the personality you want to portray. For instance, if you want your hero to be strong and powerful, opt for darker and more intense colors. If you want your hero to be playful and cheerful, go for brighter and more cheerful colors.

Textures can also add depth and interest to your crochet hero. Consider the type of yarn you're using and how it will affect the overall texture. Some yarns have a smooth and sleek texture, while others have a more fluffy and textured appearance. Experiment with different yarns to see which ones create the desired effect for your hero. For example, if you're making a hero with a furry animal companion, using a textured yarn for the animal's fur can add a realistic touch.

Additionally, consider the color and texture combinations. Certain colors and textures complement each other well, while others may clash or create a chaotic look. It's important to find a balance and harmony between the colors and textures you choose. You can create a visually pleasing result by combining contrasting colors and textures, such as pairing a smooth yarn with a textured one or using complementary colors.

Lastly, don't be afraid to experiment and try new things. Crochet heroes are a creative outlet, and the possibilities are endless. Play around with different color and texture combinations, and trust your instincts. Sometimes the most unexpected combinations can result in the most unique and eye-catching crochet heroes.

In conclusion, choosing colors and textures for your crochet heroes requires careful consideration and thought. By considering the theme, personality, and desired effect of your hero, as well as experimenting with different color and texture combinations,…

Creating a Customized Hero Based on Personal Role Models by Crochet: Creating a customized hero based on personal role models by crochet is a unique and creative way to pay tribute to the individuals who have had a significant impact on our lives. Crochet, a form of needlework that involves using a hook to create intricate patterns and designs with yarn, allows us to bring our role models to life in a tangible and meaningful way.

The process of creating a customized hero through crochet begins with selecting the role models who have inspired us the most. These role models can be anyone from historical figures to family members or even fictional characters. The key is to choose individuals who embody the qualities and values that we admire and aspire to emulate.

Once the role models have been chosen, the next step is to gather the necessary materials and tools for the crochet project. This includes selecting the appropriate yarn colors and textures that best represent the chosen role models. For example, if the role model is known for their vibrant personality, using bright and bold colors would be fitting. On the other hand, if the role model is known for their calm and composed demeanor, using softer and more muted colors would be more appropriate.

After gathering the materials, the crochet process begins. This involves following a pattern or creating one from scratch to crochet the various parts of the hero, such as the head, body, arms, and legs. Each part is carefully crafted and stitched together to create a cohesive and recognizable representation of the role model.

The customization aspect comes into play during the crochet process. This involves adding personal touches and details that are unique to the role model being depicted. For example, if the role model is known for their signature hairstyle or accessory, incorporating these elements into the crochet design would make the hero even more personalized and special.

As the crochet project nears completion, the final step is to add any finishing touches and embellishments. This can include embroidering facial features, adding buttons or beads for eyes, or even attaching small accessories that further enhance the hero's resemblance to the role model.

The end result of creating a customized hero based on personal role models by crochet is a one-of-a-kind piece of art that serves as a constant reminder of the individuals who have influenced and shaped our lives. It is a tangible representation of the qualities and values that we hold dear, and a source of inspiration and motivation to strive towards becoming the best versions of ourselves.

In addition to being a creative outlet, creating a customized hero through crochet can also be a therapeutic and meditative process.

Incorporating Signature Elements and Accessories of Crochet Heroes:
When it comes to incorporating signature elements and accessories of crochet heroes, there are numerous ways to infuse their unique style and flair into your own crochet projects. Crochet heroes are individuals who have made a significant impact in the crochet community, either through their innovative designs, exceptional skills, or their ability to inspire others with their creativity. By incorporating their signature elements and accessories into your own work, you not only pay homage to these crochet heroes but also add a touch of their distinctive style to your creations.

One way to incorporate signature elements and accessories of crochet heroes is by studying their patterns and designs. Many crochet heroes have their own line of patterns, which often feature their trademark stitches, motifs, or color combinations. By carefully examining and recreating these patterns, you can learn the techniques and styles that make these crochet heroes stand out. Whether it's the intricate lacework of a particular designer or the bold color choices of another, incorporating these signature elements into your own projects can help you capture the essence of their style.

Another way to infuse the signature elements and accessories of crochet heroes into your work is by incorporating their favorite materials or tools. Some crochet heroes have a preference for specific types of yarn, hooks, or other crochet accessories. By using the same materials or tools that they favor, you can achieve a similar look and feel in your own projects. For example, if a crochet hero is known for using a particular brand of yarn that gives their creations a soft and luxurious texture, using the same yarn in your own projects can help you achieve a similar result.

Additionally, paying attention to the finishing touches and embellishments that crochet heroes use can also help you incorporate their signature elements into your work. Many crochet heroes have a knack for adding unique and eye-catching details to their projects, such as intricate borders, decorative buttons, or personalized tags. By incorporating these finishing touches into your own creations, you can add a touch of their distinctive style and elevate your crochet projects to a whole new level.

Lastly, don't be afraid to put your own spin on the signature elements and accessories of crochet heroes. While it's important to pay homage to their style and techniques, adding your own creative touch can help make your projects truly unique. Experiment with different color combinations, modify their patterns to suit your preferences, or combine elements from multiple crochet heroes to create something entirely new. By infusing your own creativity into the signature elements and accessories of crochet heroes,…

Making a Miniature of Someone You Admire in Crochet Heroes: Crochet Heroes is a popular craft activity that allows individuals to create miniature versions of people they admire using crochet techniques. This creative and intricate process involves using yarn and a crochet hook to meticulously craft a small replica of a person, capturing their likeness and essence in a unique and personalized way.

To begin the process of making a miniature of someone you admire in crochet, you first need to gather the necessary materials. This includes selecting the appropriate yarn colors that closely match the person's hair, skin tone, and clothing. Additionally, you will need a crochet hook that is suitable for the chosen yarn weight, as well as any additional accessories or embellishments you wish to include in the final creation.

Once you have all the materials ready, the next step is to find a suitable crochet pattern or design that will serve as the foundation for your miniature. There are numerous resources available, including books, online tutorials, and even specialized crochet patterns specifically designed for creating miniature figures. It is important to choose a pattern that closely resembles the person you admire, as this will ensure a more accurate representation.

With the pattern in hand, you can now begin the process of crocheting the miniature figure. This involves following the instructions provided in the pattern, which typically include a combination of different crochet stitches and techniques. It is important to pay close attention to the details and intricacies of the pattern, as this will help in capturing the unique features and characteristics of the person you are trying to recreate.

As you progress through the crocheting process, you will gradually see the miniature figure taking shape. It is important to take your time and be patient, as crocheting intricate details can be time-consuming and require precision. This is where the true artistry of crochet comes into play, as you use your skills and creativity to bring the miniature figure to life.

Once the crocheting is complete, you can then add any additional details or embellishments to enhance the likeness of the miniature figure. This may include embroidering facial features, attaching small accessories such as glasses or jewelry, or even adding miniature props that are associated with the person you admire. These finishing touches add depth and personality to the final creation, making it even more special and meaningful.

The process of making a miniature of someone you admire in crochet is not only a fun and creative activity, but it also serves as a heartfelt tribute to the person who has inspired you.

Embroidery and Detailing for Expressive Faces of Crochet Heroes: Embroidery and detailing play a crucial role in bringing the expressive faces of crochet heroes to life. These intricate techniques add depth, personality, and emotion to the characters, making them truly captivating and endearing.

When it comes to crochet heroes, their faces are often the focal point of their design. Whether it's a cute animal, a whimsical creature, or a beloved character, the face is what draws us in and creates a connection. Embroidery allows for the creation of intricate facial features such as eyes, eyebrows, noses, and mouths, which are essential for conveying different expressions and emotions.

The art of embroidery involves using various stitches and techniques to create detailed designs on fabric. For crochet heroes, this means carefully stitching on the facial features using embroidery floss or thread. The choice of colors and stitches can greatly impact the overall look and feel of the character. For example, using a satin stitch for the eyes can create a smooth and realistic appearance, while a backstitch can add a more defined and bold outline.

Detailing goes hand in hand with embroidery, as it involves adding small elements and embellishments to enhance the overall design. This can include adding rosy cheeks, freckles, or even tiny accessories like glasses or hats.

These small details may seem insignificant, but they contribute to the overall charm and personality of the crochet hero.

Moreover, embroidery and detailing allow for customization and personalization. Each crochet hero can have its own unique facial expression, allowing the creator to convey a specific mood or personality. A mischievous smile, a curious gaze, or a friendly wink can all be achieved through the art of embroidery and detailing.

Additionally, embroidery and detailing can also be used to create texture and dimension. By using different stitches and techniques, the face of a crochet hero can have a three-dimensional quality, making it more visually appealing and lifelike. This adds depth and realism to the character, making it even more engaging and captivating.

In conclusion, embroidery and detailing are essential techniques for bringing the expressive faces of crochet heroes to life. They allow for the creation of intricate facial features, customization, and personalization, as well as adding texture and dimension. These techniques elevate the overall design, making the crochet heroes truly enchanting and unforgettable.

Adding Accessories and Props to Enhance Characters of Crochet Heroes: One way to enhance the characters of crochet heroes is by adding accessories and props. These additional elements can help to further define the personality and story of each character, making them more engaging and memorable.

Accessories can be used to reflect the interests, hobbies, or occupations of the crochet heroes. For example, a superhero character could have a cape, mask, or emblem that represents their superpowers or mission. This not only adds visual interest to the character but also helps to establish their role in the crochet hero universe.

Props, on the other hand, can be used to enhance the storytelling aspect of the crochet heroes. These can include items such as weapons, tools, or objects that are relevant to the character's story or abilities. For instance, a pirate crochet hero could have a hook hand, a treasure map, or a parrot companion. These props not only add depth to the character but also provide opportunities for imaginative play and storytelling.

In addition to reflecting the character's personality and story, accessories and props can also be used to enhance the overall aesthetic of the crochet heroes. They can add pops of color, texture, or visual interest to the design, making the characters more visually appealing and dynamic.

Furthermore, accessories and props can also serve a functional purpose in the crochet heroes' design. For example, a character with a large hat or hood can help to hide any seams or imperfections in the crochet work. Similarly, a character with a staff or cane can provide additional support and stability to the crochet hero, making them easier to pose and display.

Overall, adding accessories and props to enhance the characters of crochet heroes is a creative and effective way to bring them to life. These additional elements not only add visual interest and depth to the characters but also help to establish their personality, story, and role in the crochet hero universe. Whether it's a superhero with a cape or a pirate with a hook hand, these accessories and props can make the crochet heroes more engaging, memorable, and enjoyable for both the creator and the audience.

Techniques for Sturdy and Play-Friendly Finishes of Crochet Heroes: When it comes to creating crochet heroes, it is important to ensure that the finished product is not only visually appealing but also sturdy and play-friendly. This requires the use of specific techniques and finishes that can withstand the wear and tear of playtime while maintaining their overall integrity.

One technique that can be employed to achieve a sturdy finish is the use of tight stitches. By using smaller hooks and working the stitches tightly, the resulting fabric will be more durable and less likely to unravel or come apart. This is especially important for areas of the crochet hero that will be subjected to frequent handling, such as the limbs or the head.

In addition to tight stitches, reinforcing certain areas of the crochet hero can also contribute to its overall sturdiness. This can be done by adding extra rounds or rows of stitches to areas that are prone to stretching or tearing, such as the joints or the seams. By reinforcing these areas, the crochet hero will be better equipped to withstand the rigors of playtime and will be less likely to come apart.

Another important aspect of creating a play-friendly finish for crochet heroes is the choice of materials. Opting for yarns that are specifically designed for durability, such as acrylic or cotton blends, can greatly enhance the longevity of the finished product. These yarns are often more resistant to pilling, stretching, and fading, making them ideal for items that will be subjected to frequent use and handling.

Furthermore, the choice of finishing techniques can also contribute to the play-friendliness of the crochet hero. For example, using a slip stitch or a single crochet stitch to join pieces together can create a seamless finish that is less likely to snag or unravel during play. Additionally, weaving in all loose ends and securing them tightly will prevent any potential unraveling or fraying, ensuring that the crochet hero remains intact even after hours of play.

Lastly, considering the overall design and construction of the crochet hero can also contribute to its sturdiness and play-friendliness. For instance, incorporating reinforced stitching or additional layers of fabric in areas that will be subjected to more stress, such as the hands or feet, can help prevent tearing or unraveling. Additionally, ensuring that the stuffing is evenly distributed and securely packed will help maintain the shape and structure of the crochet hero, even during rough play.

In conclusion, creating sturdy and play-friendly finishes for crochet heroes requires a combination of techniques, materials, and design considerations. By employing tight stitches, reinforcing vulnerable areas, choosing durable materials,…

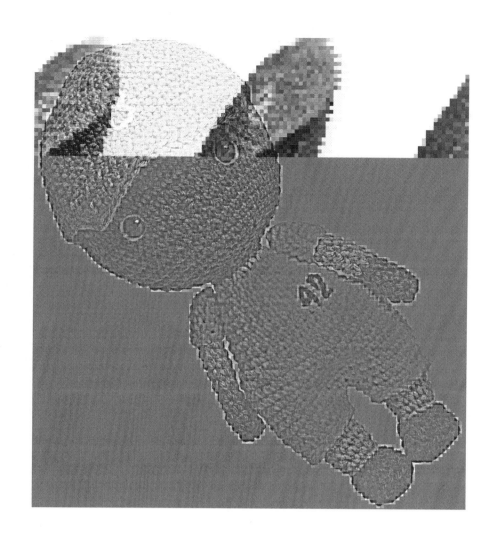

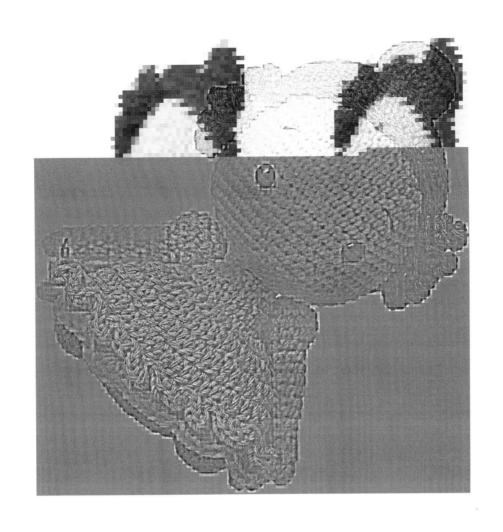

INTRODUCTION

Hello, dear crochet friend, and welcome to the world of *this book*. In the pages of this book, you will find everything you need to recreate twenty iconic heroes with colorful yarns and a crochet hook.

In the Projects section, you will meet the twenty incredible women and men who have been chosen from the many contemporary and present-day heroes I admire. During the process of creating these dolls, I got to know every one of them on a deeper level. I became familiar not only with their art, inspiration, or creativity, but also their struggles in life, and the hard work it has taken to overcome them. I've had my personal favorites, my own heroes among them, long before writing this book—but during the months I focused on these amazing artists, athletes, activists, and public figures, I managed to fall in love with each and every one of them, as I always found something that took my breath away.
From Josephine Baker's unwavering bravery during World War II and the persistence of Rosa Parks and Malala, to the pure, inevitable talent of Prince, Frida Kahlo, and Audrey Hepburn—most of these heroes were innovators and revolutionists in their field. They were ahead of their time in so many ways. But what makes them special for me, and perhaps for most of us, is that they all made a lasting difference.

In the Techniques section of the book, you will find all of the stitches and techniques needed to crochet your own heroes. Each project lists the yarn type with my color choices, but I would also encourage you to choose your very own favorite colors, or even yarn brand. When it comes to amigurumi, I always use 100% cotton yarn, but you can experiment with different types of yarn, for example, wool or acrylic.

So, grab a cup of coffee or tea, settle yourself comfortably, pick up your crochet hook, and recreate each of the heroes in this book. I hope they will bring joy and happiness to your life and, most of all, inspire you.

YOU WILL NEED

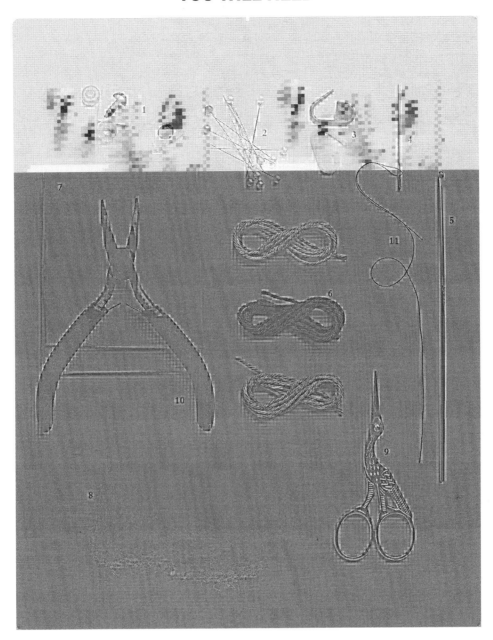

1. $^5/_{16}$" (8mm) safety eyes **2.** Pins **3.** Stitch markers **4.** Tapestry needle **5.** B–1 or C–2 (2.5 mm) crochet hook **6.** 100% cotton yarn **7.** White felt **8.** Polyfiber stuffing **9.** Scissors **10.** Round-nose pliers **11.** Black thread (See note on this page on how tools, materials, and gauge will affect the size of the finished dolls.)

Malala Yousafzai

Jane Goodall

Prince

MISTY COPELAND

Misty Copeland is a ballet dancer for the American Ballet Theatre. Despite starting to learn ballet at the relatively late age of thirteen—and being challenged by her difference— Misty became the company's first African-American soloist for two decades. At the age of thirty-two, she also became the first African-American woman to be promoted to principal dancer at the Theatre. Behind success there is often pain and suffering, and it was no different for Misty. She overcame family difficulties, health issues, and body-image struggles and went on to become a role model and pop icon.

MATERIALS

B-1 or C-2 (2.5 mm) crochet hook

$^5/_{16}$" (8 mm) safety eyes

Tapestry needle

Polyester fiberfill

Black thread for embroidery

Small amount of white felt

YARNS

Scheepjes Catona 100% cotton yarn:

507 Chocolate—skin, 20 g

105 Bridal White—dress, headpieces, 22 g

263 Petal Peach—shoes, 3 g

110 Jet Black—hair, 18 g

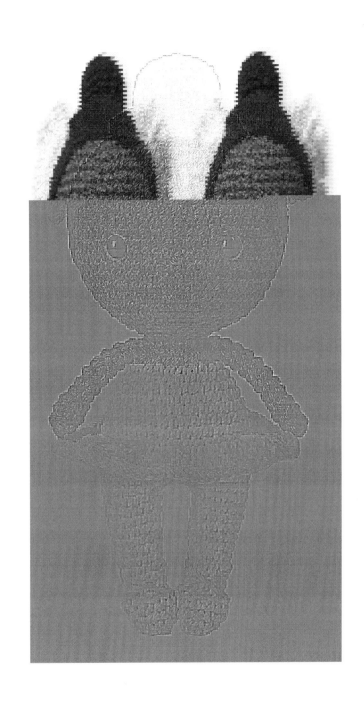

HEAD

Start with the skin color.

Rnd 1. 6 sc into magic ring (6).

Rnd 2. 2 sc into each (12).

Rnd 3. {sc, inc} 6 times (18).

Rnd 4. {sc into 2, inc} 6 times (24).

Rnd 5. {sc into 3, inc} 6 times (30).

Rnd 6. {sc into 4, inc} 6 times (36).

Rnd 7. {sc into 5, inc} 6 times (42).

Rnd 8. {sc into 6, inc} 6 times (48).

Rnd 9. {sc into 7, inc} 6 times (54).

Rnds 10–16. Sc into each (54).

Rnd 17. {sc into 8, inc} 6 times (60).

Rnds 18–20. Sc into each (60).

Rnd 21. {sc into 8, dec} 6 times (54).

Rnd 22. {sc into 7, dec} 6 times (48).

Rnd 23. {sc into 6, dec} 6 times (42).

Rnd 24. {sc into 5, dec} 6 times (36).

Add the eyes (see here for guidance).

Rnd 25. {sc into 4, dec} 6 times (30).

Rnd 26. {sc into 3, dec} 6 times (24).

Start to stuff the head.

Rnd 27. {sc into 2, dec} 6 times (18).

Rnd 28. {sc, dec} 6 times (12).

Continue to stuff the head firmly.

Rnd 29. Sc into each FLO (12).

Do not fasten off, continue with the body.

BODY

Rnd 1. {sc, inc} 6 times (18).

Rnd 2. {sc into 2, inc} 6 times (24).

Change to the color of the dress.

Rnd 3. Sc into each (24).

Rnd 4. {sc into 3, inc} 6 times (30).

Rnd 5. Sc into each (30).

Rnd 6. {sc into 4, inc} 6 times (36).

Rnds 7–10. Sc into each (36).

Rnd 11. Sc into each BLO (36).

Rnd 12. Sc into each (36).

Rnd 13. {sc into 16, dec} 2 times (34).

Rnds 14–15. Sc into each (34).

Do not fasten off, continue with the legs. Stuff the neck and body continuously.

LEGS

To make the legs, divide the work: 14 stitches for each of the legs, and 3 stitches between the legs, both front and back. Mark the stitches with yarn or a stitch marker. Make sure the legs line up with the eyes. If the last stitch of the body is within the 14 stitches for the legs, then continue crocheting. If it is within the 3 stitches, then fasten off, leave a tail for sewing later, and rejoin the dress-colored yarn with a sl st at the back of the doll.

Rnds 1–3. Sc into each (14).

Rnd 4. {sc into 5, dec} 2 times (12).

Rnds 5–6. Sc into each (12).

Stuff the body firmly and stuff the leg as you crochet it.

Rnd 7. {sc into 4, dec} 2 times (10).

Rnds 8–12. Sc into each (10).

Stuff the leg firmly.

Rnd 13. Dec 5 times (5).

Fasten off, sew up the small hole, and weave in the ends. For the second leg, rejoin with a sl st at the back of the doll and work the leg. When finished, sew up the hole between the legs. Weave in the ends.

EYEBROWS AND NOSE

Using black thread, embroider the eyebrows between rounds 12 and 14. With skin-colored yarn, embroider the nose between rounds 18 and 19.

SKIRT

Using the color of the dress, join with a sl st to a front loop of round 10 at the center back of the body. Work continuously but join with a sl st at the end of each round. Ch 2 at the beginning does not count as dc.

Rnd 1. Ch 2, 2 dc into each. Join with a sl st to first dc (72).

Rnd 2. Ch 2, dc into each. Join with a sl st to first dc (72).

Rnd 3. Sl st into each (72).

Fasten off and weave in the ends.

HAIR

Use the hair color.

Rnd 1. 6 sc into magic ring (6).

Rnd 2. 2 sc into each (12).

Rnd 3. {sc, inc} 6 times (18).

Rnd 4. {sc into 2, inc} 6 times (24).

Rnd 5. {sc into 3, inc} 6 times (30).

Rnd 6. {sc into 4, inc} 6 times (36).

Rnd 7. {sc into 5, inc} 6 times (42).

Rnd 8. {sc into 6, inc} 6 times (48).

Rnd 9. {sc into 7, inc} 6 times (54).

Rnds 10–19. Sc into each (54).

Fasten off and leave a long tail for sewing. Place the hair on the head, secure it with pins, and sew it into place.

BUN

Use the hair color.

Rnd 1. 6 sc into magic ring (6).

Rnd 2. 2 sc into each (12).

Rnd 3. {sc, inc} 6 times (18).

Rnd 4. {sc into 2, inc} 6 times (24).

Rnds 5–7. Sc into each (24).

Rnd 8. {sc into 2, dec} 6 times (18).

Fasten off and leave a long tail for sewing. Stuff the bun, then place it on the head between rounds 2 and 8 of the hair. Secure the bun with pins, and sew it into place.

ARMS

Use the skin color, make two.

Rnd 1. 6 sc into magic ring (6).

Rnd 2. {sc, inc} 3 times (9).

Rnd 3. Sc into each (9).

Rnd 4. {sc, dec} 3 times (6).

Rnds 5–11. Sc into each (6).

Fasten off and leave a long tail for sewing. Sew an arm on each side of the doll and weave in the ends.

SHOES

Use the color of the shoes, make two.

Rnd 1. 6 sc into magic ring (6).

Rnd 2. 2 sc into each (12).

Rnds 3–4. Sc into each (12).

Fasten off and leave a long tail. Place one shoe onto a leg, ensuring the long tail is on the left. Cross the tail in front of the leg upward, and using a needle, pull the yarn through a stitch at round 7 at the back. Cross the tail in front of the leg downward, and insert the needle through the shoe and the leg from right to left. Secure the shoe with a few stitches. Fasten off and weave in the ends. Sew the second shoe to the other leg in the same way.

HEADPIECES

Use the color of the headpieces, make two.

Ch 10 (foundation chain), sl st into 2nd ch from hook and into next 2. * Ch 4, sl st into 2nd ch from hook and into next 2, sl st into next st on foundation chain. Repeat from * 6 times. Fasten off, leaving a long tail.

Sew headpiece onto the hair at round 16 on one side of the head. Repeat for the other side. Weave in the ends.

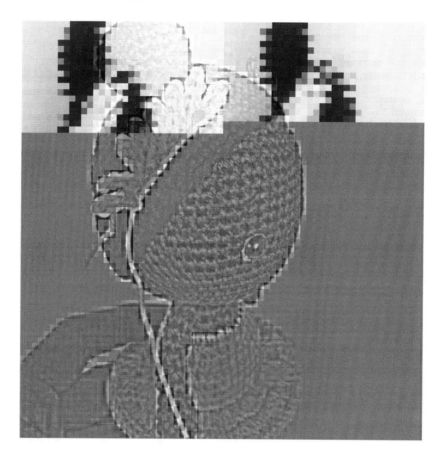

FRIDA KAHLO

Mexican artist Frida Kahlo was renowned for her self-portraits and use of vibrant colors. One of the most iconic women of the twentieth century, she is symbolic of love, passion, strength, suffering, and, most of all, art. A beautiful soul who lived her life to the fullest—displaying a deep sense of independence, rebellion, and outspoken political activism—Frida is still admired as a feminist icon today.

MATERIALS

B-1 or C-2 (2.5 mm) crochet hook

$5/16$" (8 mm) safety eyes

Tapestry needle

Polyester fiberfill

Black thread for embroidery

Extra fine merino wool—black

Small amount of white felt

YARNS

Scheepjes Catona 100% cotton yarn:

502 Camel—skin, 20 g

252 Watermelon—dress, 18 g

110 Jet Black—hair, 15 g

192 Scarlet—roses, 5 g

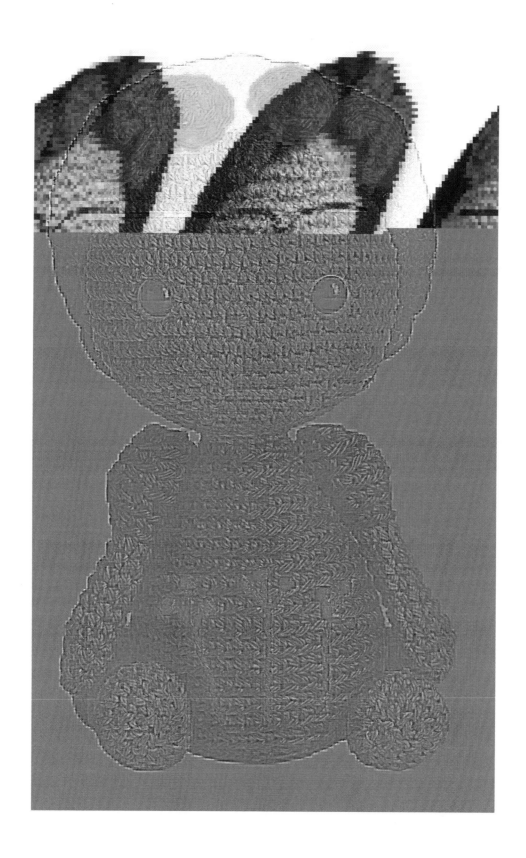

HEAD

Start with the skin color.

Rnd 1. 6 sc into magic ring (6).

Rnd 2. 2 sc into each (12).

Rnd 3. {sc, inc} 6 times (18).

Rnd 4. {sc into 2, inc} 6 times (24).

Rnd 5. {sc into 3, inc} 6 times (30).

Rnd 6. {sc into 4, inc} 6 times (36).

Rnd 7. {sc into 5, inc} 6 times (42).

Rnd 8. {sc into 6, inc} 6 times (48).

Rnd 9. {sc into 7, inc} 6 times (54).

Rnds 10–16. Sc into each (54).

Rnd 17. {sc into 8, inc} 6 times (60).

Rnds 18–20. Sc into each (60).

Rnd 21. {sc into 8, dec} 6 times (54).

Rnd 22. {sc into 7, dec} 6 times (48).

Rnd 23. {sc into 6, dec} 6 times (42).

Rnd 24. {sc into 5, dec} 6 times (36).

Add the eyes (see here for guidance).

Rnd 25. {sc into 4, dec} 6 times (30).

Rnd 26. {sc into 3, dec} 6 times (24).

Start to stuff the head.

Rnd 27. {sc into 2, dec} 6 times (18).

Rnd 28. {sc, dec} 6 times (12).

Continue to stuff the head firmly.

Rnd 29. Sc into each FLO (12).

Change to the color of the dress.

BODY

From round 2 crochet into BLO throughout the body.

Rnd 1. {sc, inc} 6 times (18).

Rnd 2. BLO {sc into 2, inc} 6 times (24).

Rnd 3. BLO sc into each (24).

Rnd 4. BLO {sc into 3, inc} 6 times (30).

Rnds 5–6. BLO sc into each (30).

Rnd 7. BLO {sc into 4, inc} 6 times (36).

Rnds 8–9. BLO sc into each (36).

Rnd 10. BLO {sc into 5, inc} 6 times (42).

Rnds 11–15. BLO sc into each (42).

Rnd 16. BLO {sc into 5, dec} 6 times (36).

Start to stuff the neck and body continuously.

Rnd 17. BLO sc into each (36).

Rnd 18. BLO {sc into 4, dec} 6 times (30).

Rnd 19. BLO {sc into 3, dec} 6 times (24).

Rnd 20. BLO {sc into 2, dec} 6 times (18).

Stuff the body firmly.

Rnd 21. BLO {sc, dec} 6 times (12).

Rnd 22. BLO dec 6 times (6).

Fasten off and leave a long tail for sewing. Sew up the hole and weave in the ends.

EYEBROWS AND NOSE

Position two pins for the nose placement between rounds 18 and 19, and embroider the nose with skin-colored yarn. For the eyebrows, place five pins between rounds 12 and 13. Follow the pictures to place the pins and embroider the eyebrows with black thread. Embroider a "V" shape directly above the nose. You can add a cheek blush with makeup or watercolor pencil.

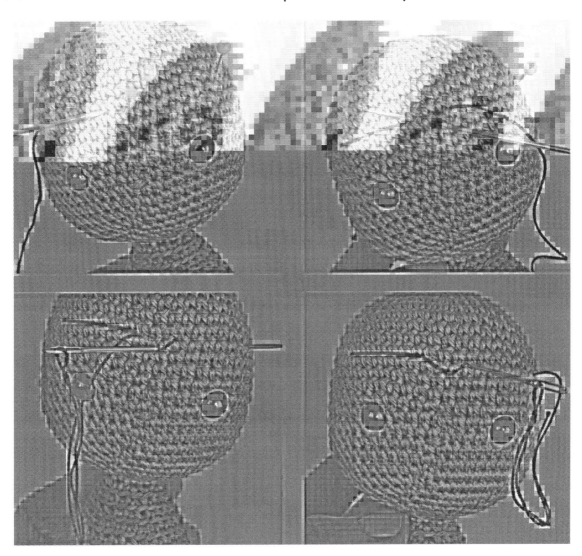

HAIR

Use the hair color.

Rnd 1. 6 sc into magic ring (6).
Rnd 2. 2 sc into each (12).
Rnd 3. {sc, inc} 6 times (18).
Rnd 4. {sc into 2, inc} 6 times (24).
Rnd 5. {sc into 3, inc} 6 times (30).
Rnd 6. {sc into 4, inc} 6 times (36).
Rnd 7. {sc into 5, inc} 6 times (42).
Rnd 8. {sc into 6, inc} 6 times (48).
Rnd 9. {sc into 7, inc} 6 times (54).
Rnds 10–17. Sc into each (54).
Rnd 18. Sc into 45, hdc into 7, sl st into 2 (54).
Rnd 19. Hdc into 7, sl st into 2.

Fasten off and leave a long tail for sewing. Place the hair on the head, secure it with pins, and sew it into place.

BRAID

Using three pieces of black merino wool, make a braid about 10" (25 cm) long. Place it around the head, secure it with pins, and using small stitches, sew it onto the hair.

ROSES

Use the color of the roses, make four.

Ch 11, turn, 2 sc into 2nd ch from hook and into next 9 (20). Fasten off and leave a long tail for sewing. Roll up and sew the bottom edges together with a few stitches. Place the roses onto the hair and sew into position.

LEGS

Start with the color of the dress, make two.

Rnd 1. 6 sc into magic ring (6).

Rnd 2. BLO 2 sc into each (12).

Rnd 3. BLO {sc into 2, inc} 4 times (16).

Rnds 4–5. BLO sc into each (16).

Rnd 6. BLO {sc into 2, dec} 4 times (12).

Rnd 7. BLO sc into each (12).

Change to the skin color.

Rnd 8. BLO sc into each (12).

Rnds 9–11. Sc into each (12).

Rnd 12. Inc 2 times, sc into 10 (14).

Rnd 13. Inc 4 times, sc into 10 (18).

Rnds 14–15. Sc into each (18).

Start to stuff the leg.

Rnd 16. Dec 9 times (9).

Rnd 17. Dec 3 more times.

Stuff the toe of the leg. Fasten off and leave a long tail for sewing. Sew up the hole and weave in the ends. Position a leg on each side of the doll and sew them into place.

DRESS EMBROIDERY

Using black thread, embroider three flowers onto the front of the dress. You will use basic stitches for the stems and French knots for the blossoms. Pull the needle through between rounds 14 and 15 of the body, and then thread it through four front loops, working upward and to the left in a straight line. Then, working downward, pull the needle from right to left through each black stitch between the front loops of the body. Do this all the way down to produce a black line. Then insert the needle into the starting point and pull it back out at the top of the stem. Mark the places for the offshoots with three pins and embroider them continuously. Position a French knot (see here) at the end of each offshoot. Do not fasten off after each flower; instead continue to embroider the middle and final flowers onto the dress in the same way.

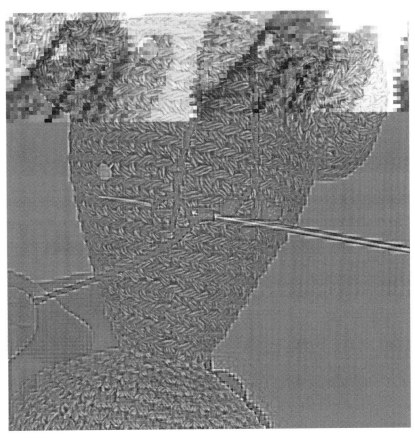

Dress embroidery

ARMS

Start with the color of the dress, make two.

Rnd 1. 6 sc into magic ring (6).

Rnd 2. BLO {sc, inc} 3 times (9).

Rnd 3. BLO {sc into 2, inc} 3 times (12).

Rnd 4. BLO sc into each (12).

Rnd 5. BLO {sc, dec} 4 times (8).

Rnd 6. BLO sc into each (8).

Slightly stuff the upper part of the arms. Change to the skin color.

Rnd 7. BLO sc into each (8).

Rnds 8–11. Sc into each (8).

Rnd 12. {sc into 2, inc} 2 times, sc into last 2 (10).

Rnds 13–14. Sc into each (10).

Rnd 15. Dec 5 times (5).

Fasten off and leave a long tail for sewing. Sew up the hole and weave in the ends. Position an arm on each side of the doll and sew them into place.

FRENCH KNOTS

1. Pull the needle through to the front of the crochet where you want to place the French knot.

2. Holding your needle in one hand, use your other hand to wrap the thread around the needle 2 times, keeping the thread as taut as possible.

3. Insert the needle back into the crochet fabric (while holding the thread tightly) as close to your original starting point as possible, and pull the needle and the thread through to the next marker—while holding the thread taut. Try to avoid using the same hole because you will pull the knot through to the wrong side.

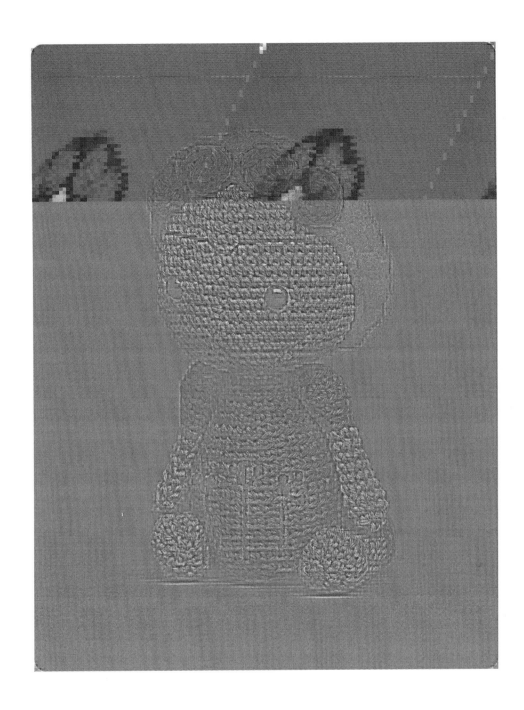

RITA MORENO

Rita Moreno is a Puerto Rican actress, dancer, and singer. What's not to love about a woman who said Marlon Brando was the "lust of her life"? She is one of the few artists to have won all four major American entertainment awards: an Emmy, a Grammy, an Oscar, and a Tony. She was the first Latina actress to win an Oscar for her performance in *West Side Story*. In her nearly seventy-year career, Moreno has never stopped fighting against typecasting and for fair representation of Latinos. She returned to the stage aged eighty with her biographical one-woman show, which became a Broadway sensation.

MATERIALS

B-1 or C-2 (2.5 mm) crochet hook

$^5/_{16}$" (8 mm) safety eyes

Tapestry needle

Polyester fiberfill

Black thread for embroidery

Small amount of white felt

YARNS

Scheepjes Catona 100% cotton yarn:

505 Linen—skin, 22 g

110 Jet Black—dress, gloves, 25 g

162 Black Coffee—hair, 20 g

383 Ginger Gold—flowers, shoes, 20 g

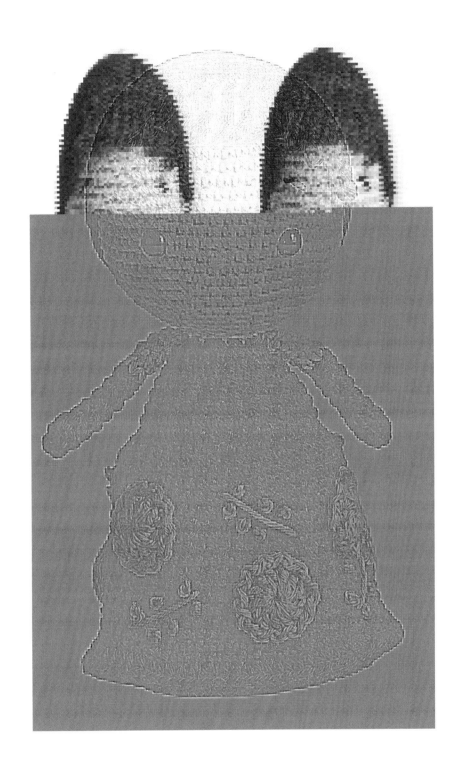

HEAD

Start with the skin color.

Rnd 1. 6 sc into magic ring (6).

Rnd 2. 2 sc into each (12).

Rnd 3. {sc, inc} 6 times (18).

Rnd 4. {sc into 2, inc} 6 times (24).

Rnd 5. {sc into 3, inc} 6 times (30).

Rnd 6. {sc into 4, inc} 6 times (36).

Rnd 7. {sc into 5, inc} 6 times (42).

Rnd 8. {sc into 6, inc} 6 times (48).

Rnd 9. {sc into 7, inc} 6 times (54).

Rnds 10–16. Sc into each (54).

Rnd 17. {sc into 8, inc} 6 times (60).

Rnds 18–20. Sc into each (60).

Rnd 21. {sc into 8, dec} 6 times (54).

Rnd 22. {sc into 7, dec} 6 times (48).

Rnd 23. {sc into 6, dec} 6 times (42).

Rnd 24. {sc into 5, dec} 6 times (36).

Add the eyes (see here for guidance).

Rnd 25. {sc into 4, dec} 6 times (30).

Rnd 26. {sc into 3, dec} 6 times (24).

Start to stuff the head.

Rnd 27. {sc into 2, dec} 6 times (18).

Rnd 28. {sc, dec} 6 times (12).

Continue to stuff the head firmly.

Rnd 29. Sc into each FLO (12).

Change to the color of the dress.

BODY

Rnd 1. {sc, inc} 6 times (18).

Rnd 2. {sc into 2, inc} 6 times (24).

Rnd 3. Sc into each (24).

Rnd 4. {sc into 3, inc} 6 times (30).

Rnd 5. Sc into each (30).

Rnd 6. {sc into 4, inc} 6 times (36).

Rnds 7–9. Sc into each (36).

Rnd 10. Sc into each BLO (36).

Rnds 11–12. Sc into each (36).

Rnd 13. {sc into 16, dec} 2 times (34).

Rnds 14–15. Sc into each (34).

Fasten off and weave in the ends. Stuff the neck and body continuously.

LEGS

To make the legs, divide the work: 14 stitches for each of the legs, and 3 stitches between the legs, both front and back. Mark the stitches with yarn or a stitch marker. Make sure the legs line up with the eyes. Use skin-colored yarn and join with a sl st at the back of the doll to start.

Rnds 1–3. Sc into each (14).

Rnd 4. {sc into 5, dec} 2 times (12).

Rnds 5–8. Sc into each (12).

Stuff the body firmly and stuff the leg as you crochet it.

Rnd 9. {sc into 4, dec} 2 times (10).

Rnds 10–12. Sc into each (10).

Stuff the leg firmly.

Rnd 13. Dec 5 times (5).

Fasten off, sew up the small hole, and weave in the ends. For the second leg, rejoin with a sl st at the back of the doll and work the leg. When finished, use black yarn to sew up the hole between the legs. Weave in the ends.

SKIRT

Using the color of the dress, join with a sl st to a front loop of round 9 at the center back of the body. Work continuously but join with a sl st at the end of each round. Ch 1 at the beginning does not count as sc.

Rnd 1. Ch 1, {sc, inc} 18 times (54).

Rnds 2–17. Ch 1, sc into each (54).

Rnd 18. Ch 1, {hdc, inc} 27 times (81).

Rnd 19. Sl st into each (81).

Fasten off and weave in the ends.

EYEBROWS AND NOSE

Using black thread, embroider the eyebrows between rounds 12 and 14. With skin-colored yarn, embroider the nose between rounds 18 and 19. You can add a cheek blush with makeup or watercolor pencil.

FLOWERS

Use the color of the flowers, make six.

Rnd 1. 12 dc into magic ring (12).

Rnd 2. {ch 1, sl st into next} 12 times.

Fasten off and leave a long tail for sewing. Evenly space the flowers on the skirt, pin, and sew them into place. Embroider lines, $^{13}/_{16}$" (2 cm) long, between the flowers. Embroider three dots on both sides of the lines using French knots (see here).

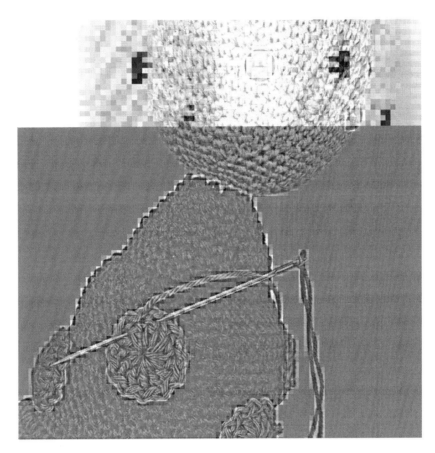

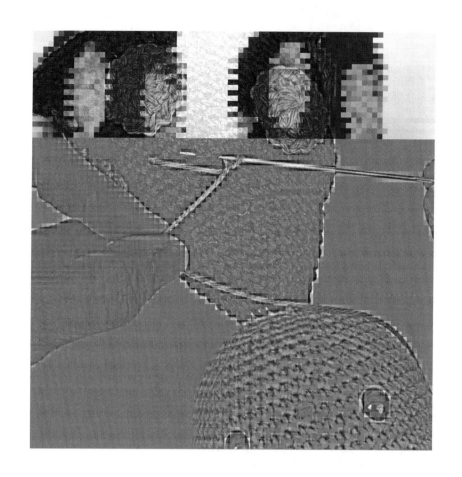

HAIR

Use the hair color.

Rnd 1. 6 sc into magic ring (6).

Rnd 2. 2 sc into each (12).

Rnd 3. {sc, inc} 6 times (18).

Rnd 4. {sc into 2, inc} 6 times (24).

Rnd 5. {sc into 3, inc} 6 times (30).

Rnd 6. {sc into 4, inc} 6 times (36).

Rnd 7. {sc into 5, inc} 6 times (42).

Rnd 8. {sc into 6, inc} 6 times (48).

Rnd 9. {sc into 7, inc} 6 times (54).

Rnds 10–16. Sc into each (54).

Rnd 17. Dc into 20, sc into next, sl st into next, ch 9, sl st into 2nd ch from hook and next 7, sl st into next on the wig. * Ch 7, sl st into 2nd ch from hook and next 5, sl st into next on the wig. Repeat from * 9 times. Ch 9, sl st into 2nd ch from hook and next 7, sl st into next on the wig. Sc into next on the wig, dc into last 20 on the wig. Fasten off and leave a long tail for sewing. Place the hair on the head, secure it with pins, and sew it into place.

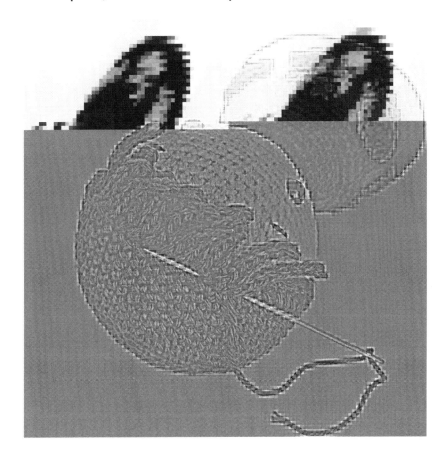

BUN

Use the hair color.

Rnd 1. 6 sc into magic ring (6).

Rnd 2. 2 sc into each (12).

Rnd 3. {sc, inc} 6 times (18).

Rnd 4. {sc into 2, inc} 6 times (24).

Rnd 5. {sc into 3, inc} 6 times (30).

Rnd 6. {sc into 4, inc} 6 times (36).

Rnds 7–9. Sc into each (36).

Rnd 10. {sc into 4, dec} 6 times (30).

Fasten off and leave a long tail for sewing. Stuff the bun, then place it on the head between rounds 6 and 17 of the hair. Secure the bun with pins, and sew it into place.

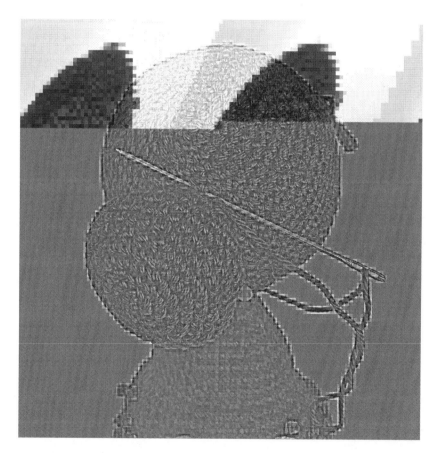

SHOES

Use the color of the shoes, make two.

Rnd 1. Ch 4, 2 sc into 2nd ch from hook, sc, 3 sc into next. Continue working on the other side of the foundation chain: sc, 2 sc into last (9).

Rnd 2. Inc 2 times, sc, inc 3 times, sc, inc 2 times (16).

Rnd 3. Sc into each BLO (16).

Rnd 4. Sc into 5, dec 3 times, sc into 5 (13).

Rnd 5. Sc into 6, dec, sc into 5 (12).

Fasten off and leave a long tail for sewing. Add stuffing to the toe of the shoes, position them on the legs, and sew them into place. Weave in the ends.

ARMS

Start with the color of the gloves, make two.

Rnd 1. 6 sc into magic ring (6).

Rnd 2. {sc, inc} 3 times (9).

Rnd 3. Sc into each (9).

Rnd 4. {sc, dec} 3 times (6).

Rnds 5–8. Sc into each (6).

Change to the skin color.

Rnd 9. Sc into each BLO (6).

Rnds 10–12. Sc into each (6).

Fasten off and leave a long tail for sewing. Position an arm on each side of the doll and sew them into place. Weave in the ends.

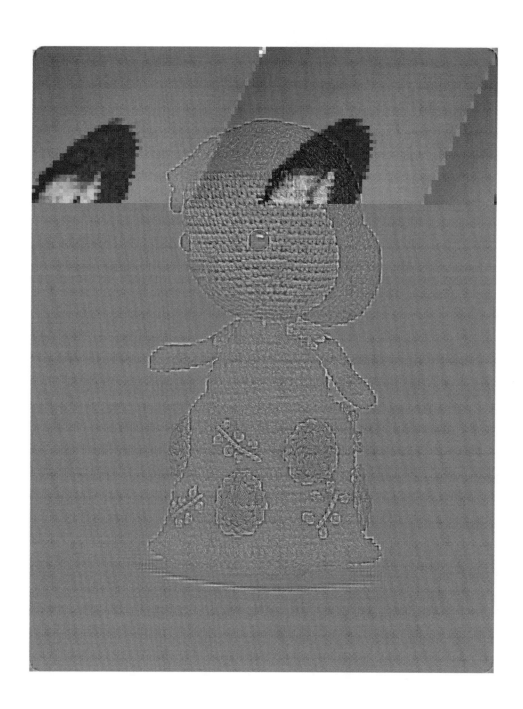

COCO CHANEL

Gabrielle "Coco" Chanel was a French fashion designer and businesswoman. Regarded as an entrepreneur and polymath, a lesser known fact about her is that she designed the double-C logo for her brand—a logo that has been in use since the 1920s. She is admired and loved for several reasons. She was an innovator, establishing a new standard of style that liberated women from corsets; she founded the famous casual-chic style; and she invented the little black dress, the Chanel suit, and the iconic fragrance, Chanel No. 5.

MATERIALS

B-1 or C-2 (2.5 mm) crochet hook

$5/16$" (8 mm) safety eyes

Tapestry needle

Polyester fiberfill

Black thread for embroidery

Small amount of white felt

YARNS

Scheepjes Catona 100% cotton yarn:

130 Old Lace—skin, 22 g

110 Jet Black—hair, skirt, 25 g

106 Snow White—shirt, 5 g

164 Light Navy—shirt, 10 g

502 Camel—hat, shoes, 10 g

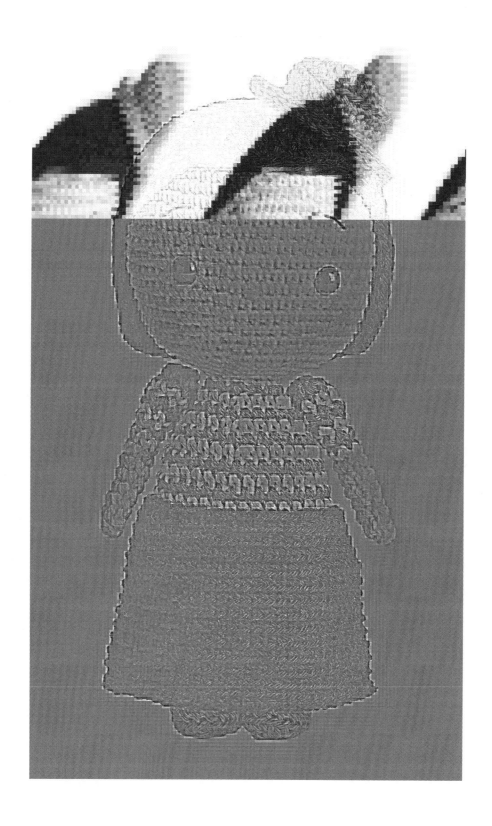

HEAD

Start with the skin color.

Rnd 1. 6 sc into magic ring (6).

Rnd 2. 2 sc into each (12).

Rnd 3. {sc, inc} 6 times (18).

Rnd 4. {sc into 2, inc} 6 times (24).

Rnd 5. {sc into 3, inc} 6 times (30).

Rnd 6. {sc into 4, inc} 6 times (36).

Rnd 7. {sc into 5, inc} 6 times (42).

Rnd 8. {sc into 6, inc} 6 times (48).

Rnd 9. {sc into 7, inc} 6 times (54).

Rnds 10–16. Sc into each (54).

Rnd 17. {sc into 8, inc} 6 times (60).

Rnds 18–20. Sc into each (60).

Rnd 21. {sc into 8, dec} 6 times (54).

Rnd 22. {sc into 7, dec} 6 times (48).

Rnd 23. {sc into 6, dec} 6 times (42).

Rnd 24. {sc into 5, dec} 6 times (36).

Add the eyes (see here for guidance).

Rnd 25. {sc into 4, dec} 6 times (30).

Rnd 26. {sc into 3, dec} 6 times (24).

Start to stuff the head.

Rnd 27. {sc into 2, dec} 6 times (18).

Rnd 28. {sc, dec} 6 times (12).

Continue to stuff the head firmly.

Rnd 29. Sc into each FLO (12).

Change to the blue shirt yarn.

BODY

Work continuously, but join with a sl st into the first st at the end of each round. Start with the blue yarn and change color at the end of each round.

Rnd 1. {sc, inc} 6 times (18). Change to white.

Rnd 2. {sc into 2, inc} 6 times (24). Change to blue.

Rnd 3. Sc into each (24). Change to white.

Rnd 4. {sc into 3, inc} 6 times (30). Change to blue.

Rnd 5. Sc into each (30). Change to white.

Rnd 6. {sc into 4, inc} 6 times (36). Change to blue.

Rnd 7. Sc into each (36). Change to white.

Rnd 8. Sc into each (36). Change to blue.

Rnd 9. Sc into each (36). Change to white.

Rnd 10. Sc into each (36).

Change to blue, fasten off white.

Rnd 11. Sc into each BLO (36).

Rnd 12. Sc into each (36).

Rnd 13. {sc into 16, dec} 2 times (34).

Rnds 14–15. Sc into each (34).

Fasten off and weave in the ends. Stuff the neck and body continuously.

LEGS

To make the legs, divide the work: 14 stitches for each of the legs, and 3 stitches between the legs, both front and back. Mark the stitches with yarn or a stitch marker. Make sure the legs line up with the eyes. Use skin-colored yarn and join with a sl st at the back of the doll to start.

Rnds 1–3. Sc into each (14).

Rnd 4. {sc into 5, dec} 2 times (12).

Rnds 5–8. Sc into each (12).

Stuff the body firmly and stuff the leg as you crochet it.

Rnd 9. {sc into 4, dec} 2 times (10).

Rnds 10–12. Sc into each (10).

Stuff the leg firmly.

Rnd 13. Dec 5 times (5).

Fasten off, sew up the small hole, and weave in the ends. For the second leg, rejoin with a sl st at the back of the doll and work the leg. When finished, use blue yarn to sew up the hole between the legs. Weave in the ends.

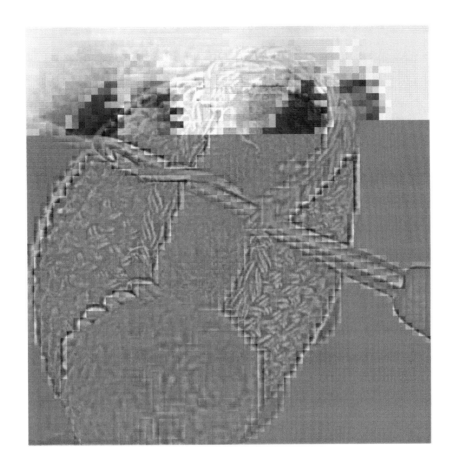

SKIRT

Using the color of the skirt, join with a sl st to a front loop of round 10 at the center back of the body. Work continuously, but join with a sl st at the end of each round. Ch 1 at the beginning does not count as sc.

Rnd 1. Ch 1, {sc into 2, inc} 12 times (48).

Rnd 2. Ch 1, BLO sc into each (48).

Rnd 3. Ch 1, BLO {sc into 5, inc} 8 times (56).

Rnds 4–14. Ch 1, BLO sc into each (56).

Rnd 15. Ch 1, sl st into each (56).

Fasten off and weave in the ends.

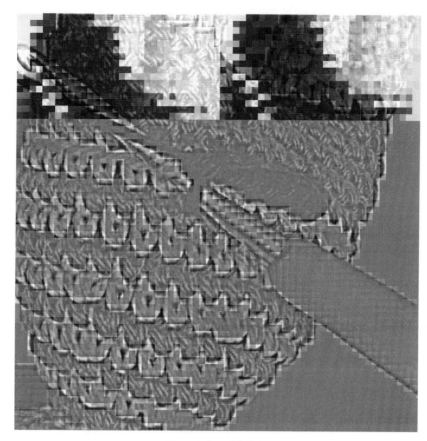

Round 1, Skirt

EYEBROWS AND NOSE

Using black thread, embroider the eyebrows between rounds 12 and 14. With skin-colored yarn, embroider the nose between rounds 18 and 19. You can add a cheek blush with makeup or watercolor pencil.

SHOES

Use the color of the shoes, make two.

Rnd 1. Ch 4, 2 sc into 2nd ch from hook, sc, 3 sc into next. Continue working on the other side of the foundation chain: sc, 2 sc into last (9).

Rnd 2. Inc 2 times, sc, inc 3 times, sc, inc 2 times (16).

Rnd 3. Sc into each BLO (16).

Rnd 4. Sc into 5, dec 3 times, sc into 5 (13).

Rnd 5. Sc into 6, dec, sc into 5 (12).

Fasten off and leave a long tail for sewing. Add stuffing to the toe of the shoes, position them on the legs, and sew them into place. Weave in the ends.

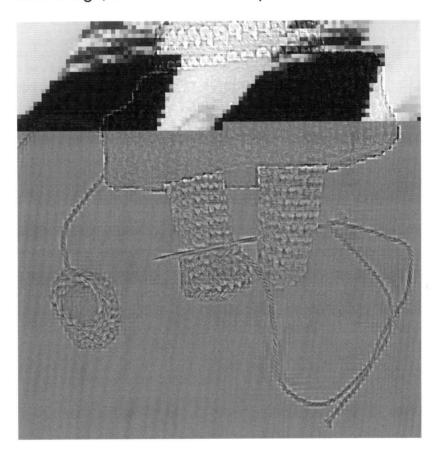

HAIR

Use the hair color.

Rnd 1. 6 sc into magic ring (6).

Rnd 2. 2 sc into each (12).

Rnd 3. {sc, inc} 6 times (18).

Rnd 4. {sc into 2, inc} 6 times (24).

Rnd 5. {sc into 3, inc} 6 times (30).

Rnd 6. {sc into 4, inc} 6 times (36).

Rnd 7. {sc into 5, inc} 6 times (42).

Rnd 8. {sc into 6, inc} 6 times (48).

Rnd 9. {sc into 7, inc} 6 times (54).

Rnds 10–11. Sc into each (54).

Rnd 12. Hdc into 8, sc into 8, hdc into 8, sc into 10, hdc into 8, sc into 4, hdc into 4, sc into 4 (54).

Rnd 13. Hdc into 10, sc into 5, hdc into 10, sc into 8, hdc into 10, sc into 2, hdc into 6, sc into 3 (54).

Rnd 14. Hdc into 8, sc into 8, hdc into 8, sc into 10, hdc into 8, sc into 3, hdc into 5, sc into 4 (54).

Rnd 15. Hdc into 8, sc into 8, hdc into 3, 3 hdc into next, hdc into 4, sc into 10, hdc into 4, 3 hdc into next, hdc into 3, sc into 5, hdc into 4, sc into 3 (58).

Rnd 16. Hdc into 8, sc into 8, hdc into 3, 3 hdc into next, hdc into 6, sc into 10, hdc into 6, 3 hdc into next, hdc into 3, sc into 4, hdc into 4, sc into 4 (62).

Rnd 17. Hdc into 6, sc into 10, hdc into 3, 3 hdc into next, hdc into 3, sc into 20, hdc into 3, 3 hdc into next, hdc into 3, sc into 4, hdc into 4, sc into 2, sl st into 2 (66).

Rnd 18. Sl st into each (66).

Fasten off and leave a long tail for sewing. Place the hair on the head, secure it with pins, and sew it into place.

ARMS

Start with blue shirt yarn, make two.

Work in continuous rounds. From rounds 2 to 5, change color at the end of each round.

Rnd 1. 6 sc into magic ring (6).

Rnd 2. {sc, inc} 3 times (9). Change to white.

Rnd 3. Sc into each (9). Change to blue.

Rnd 4. Sc into each (9). Change to white.

Rnd 5. {sc into 2, dec} 2 times, sc into last (7).

Change to blue, fasten off white. Stuff the upper part of the arm slightly.

Rnd 6. Sc into each (7).

Change to skin color, fasten off blue.

Rnds 7–11. Sc into each (7).

Rnd 12. {sc, inc} 3 times, sc into last (10).

Rnd 13. Dec 5 times (5).

Fasten off and leave a long tail for sewing. Sew up the small hole and weave in the ends. Position an arm on each side of the doll and sew them into place.

HAT

Use the color of the hat.

Rnd 1. 7 sc into magic ring (7).

Rnd 2. 2 sc into each (14).

Rnd 3. {sc, inc} 7 times (21).

Rnd 4. {sc into 6, inc} 3 times (24).

Rnd 5. Sc into each BLO (24).

Rnds 6–7. Sc into each (24).

Rnd 8. {sc, inc} 12 times (36).

Rnd 9. Sc into each (36).

Rnd 10. Sl st into each (36).

Fasten off and weave in the ends. With the same yarn, sew the hat onto the left side of the head.

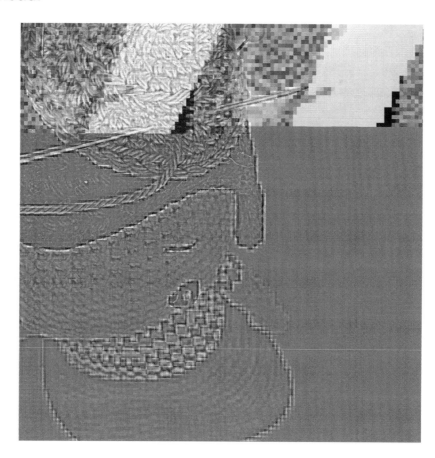

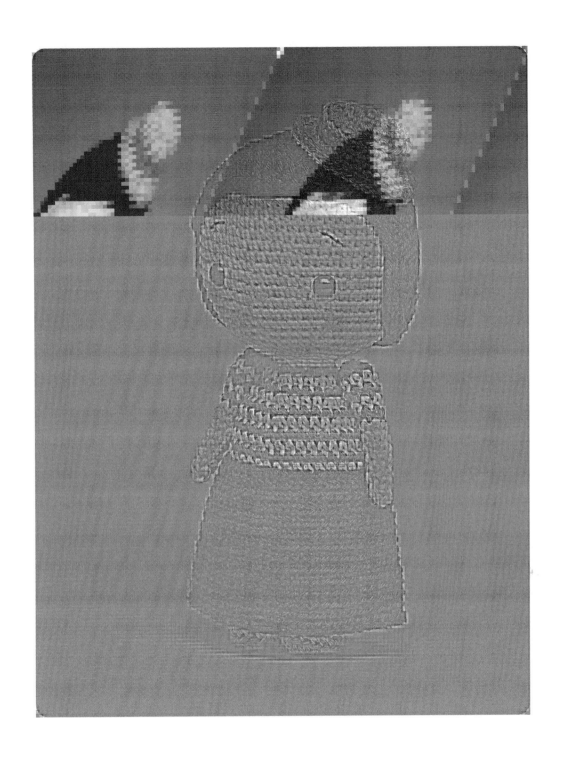

JOSEPHINE BAKER

Josephine Baker was an American-born French entertainer and civil rights activist. After a few years of dancing in New York City, she moved to Paris at the age of nineteen and became the most famous American performer in France. She revolutionized onstage performance with her erotic dancing and unusual costumes, and was also known for having a pet cheetah named Chiquita. She was multitalented, recognized not only for her dancing, but also for singing and acting.

During World War II she worked with the French Resistance, and later became involved with the American civil rights movement. Ernest Hemingway called her "the most sensational woman anyone ever saw."

MATERIALS

B-1 or C-2 (2.5 mm) crochet hook

$^5/_{16}$" (8 mm) safety eyes

Tapestry needle

Polyester fiberfill

Black thread for embroidery

Small amount of white felt

YARNS

Scheepjes Catona 100% cotton yarn:

507 Chocolate—skin, 25 g

522 Primrose—dress, 15 g

110 Jet Black—hair, shoes, 18 g

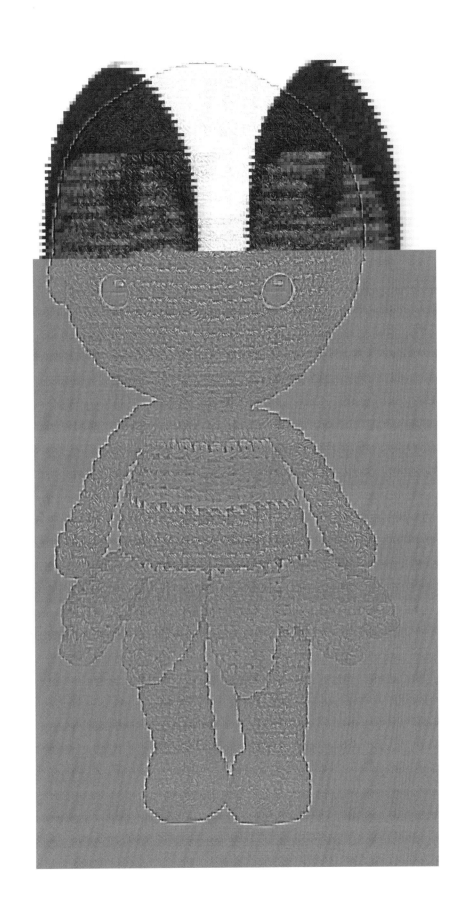

HEAD

Start with the skin color.

Rnd 1. 6 sc into magic ring (6).

Rnd 2. 2 sc into each (12).

Rnd 3. {sc, inc} 6 times (18).

Rnd 4. {sc into 2, inc} 6 times (24).

Rnd 5. {sc into 3, inc} 6 times (30).

Rnd 6. {sc into 4, inc} 6 times (36).

Rnd 7. {sc into 5, inc} 6 times (42).

Rnd 8. {sc into 6, inc} 6 times (48).

Rnd 9. {sc into 7, inc} 6 times (54).

Rnds 10–16. Sc into each (54).

Rnd 17. {sc into 8, inc} 6 times (60).

Rnds 18–20. Sc into each (60).

Rnd 21. {sc into 8, dec} 6 times (54).

Rnd 22. {sc into 7, dec} 6 times (48).

Rnd 23. {sc into 6, dec} 6 times (42).

Rnd 24. {sc into 5, dec} 6 times (36).

Add the eyes (see here for guidance).

Rnd 25. {sc into 4, dec} 6 times (30).

Rnd 26. {sc into 3, dec} 6 times (24).

Start to stuff the head.

Rnd 27. {sc into 2, dec} 6 times (18).

Rnd 28. {sc, dec} 6 times (12).

Continue to stuff the head firmly.

Rnd 29. Sc into each FLO (12).

Do not fasten off, continue with the body.

BODY

Rnd 1. {sc, inc} 6 times (18).

Rnd 2. {sc into 2, inc} 6 times (24). Change to the color of the dress.

Rnd 3. Sc into each (24).

Rnd 4. BLO {sc into 3, inc} 6 times (30).

Rnd 5. BLO sc into each (30).

Rnd 6. BLO {sc into 4, inc} 6 times (36). Change to the skin color.

Rnd 7. BLO sc into each (36).

Rnds 8–10. Sc into each (36).

Change to the color of the dress.

Rnd 11. Sc into each (36).

Rnd 12. BLO sc into each (36).

Rnd 13. BLO {sc into 16, dec} 2 times (34).

Rnds 14–15. BLO sc into each (34).

Fasten off and weave in the ends. Stuff the neck and body continuously.

LEGS

To make the legs, divide the work: 14 stitches for each of the legs, and 3 stitches between the legs, both front and back. Mark the stitches with yarn or a stitch marker. Make sure the legs line up with the eyes. Use skin-colored yarn and join with a sl st at the back of the doll to start.

Rnds 1–3. Sc into each (14).

Rnd 4. {sc into 5, dec} 2 times (12).

Rnds 5–8. Sc into each (12).

Stuff the body firmly and stuff the leg as you crochet it.

Rnd 9. {sc into 4, dec} 2 times (10).

Rnds 10–12. Sc into each (10).

Stuff the leg firmly.

Rnd 13. Dec 5 times (5).

Fasten off, sew up the small hole, and weave in the ends. For the second leg, rejoin with a sl st at the back of the doll and work the leg. When finished, use yellow yarn to sew up the hole between the legs. Weave in the ends.

EYEBROWS AND NOSE

Using black thread, embroider the eyebrows between rounds 12 and 14. With skin-colored yarn, embroider the nose between rounds 18 and 19.

SHOES

Use the color of the shoes, make two.

Rnd 1. Ch 4, 2 sc into 2nd ch from hook, sc, 3 sc into next. Continue working on the other side of the foundation chain: sc, 2 sc into last (9).

Rnd 2. Inc 2 times, sc, inc 3 times, sc, inc 2 times (16).

Rnd 3. Sc into each BLO (16).

Rnd 4. Sc into 5, dec 3 times, sc into 5 (13).

Rnd 5. Sc into 6, dec, sc into 5 (12).

Fasten off and leave a long tail for sewing. Add stuffing to the toe of the shoes, position them on the legs, and sew them into place. Weave in the ends.

SKIRT PETALS

Use the color of the dress, make nine.

Rnd 1. 6 sc into magic ring (6).

Rnd 2. {sc into 2, inc} 2 times (8).

Rnd 3. {sc into 3, inc} 2 times (10).

Rnds 4–6. Sc into each (10).

Rnd 7. {sc into 3, dec} 2 times (8).

Rnd 8. Sc into 2, sl st into next.

Fasten off and leave a long tail for sewing. Evenly space the petals on the first round of the panties, secure them with pins, and sew them into place.

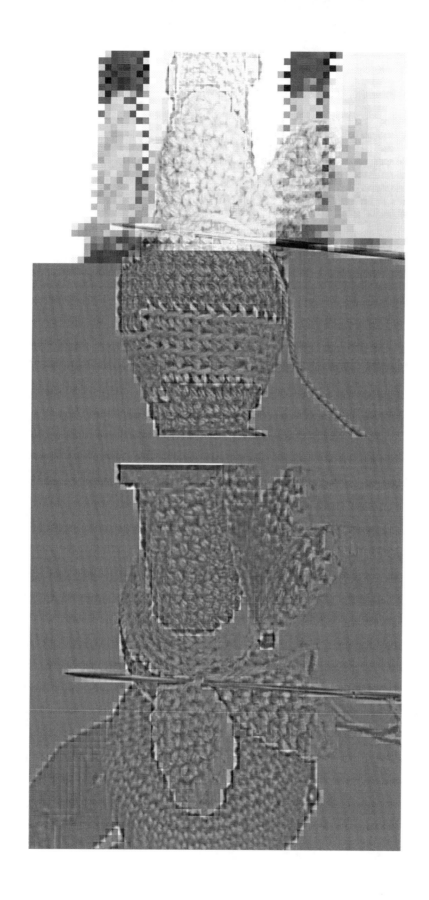

ARMS

Use the skin color, make two.

Rnd 1. 6 sc into magic ring (6).

Rnd 2. {sc, inc} 3 times (9).

Rnd 3. Sc into each (9).

Rnd 4. {sc, dec} 3 times (6).

Rnds 5–12. Sc into each (6).

Fasten off and leave a long tail for sewing. Position an arm on each side of the doll and sew them into place.

HAIR

Use the hair color.

Rnd 1. 6 sc into magic ring (6).

Rnd 2. 2 sc into each (12).

Rnd 3. {sc, inc} 6 times (18).

Rnd 4. {sc into 2, inc} 6 times (24).

Rnd 5. {sc into 3, inc} 6 times (30).

Rnd 6. {sc into 4, inc} 6 times (36).

Rnd 7. {sc into 5, inc} 6 times (42).

Rnd 8. {sc into 6, inc} 6 times (48).

Rnd 9. {sc into 7, inc} 6 times (54).

Rnds 10–17. Sc into each (54).

Rnd 18. Sc, sl st into next 2, hdc into next 2, dc into next 40, hdc into next 4, ch 7, turn, sl st into 2nd ch from hook and into next, dec, sl st into next 2, 3 sc into next on the wig, hdc into next 3.

Rnd 19. Sc, sl st into next 2, hdc into next 7, ch 9, turn, sl st into 2nd ch from hook and into next, sc into next 2, hdc into next, sc into next 2, sl st into last of ch 9. Sc into next on the wig, sc into next 10, ch 6, turn, sl st into 2nd ch from hook and into next, sc into next 2, sl st into last of ch 6. Sc into next 2 on the wig, sl st into next 5.

Fasten off and leave a long tail for sewing. Place the hair on the head, secure it with pins, and sew it into place. Sew the locks onto the head.

MAYA ANGELOU

Maya Angelou was an American autobiographer, poet, actress, screenwriter, dancer, composer, and activist. She is perhaps best known for her 1969 memoir *I Know Why the Caged Bird Sings*—the first nonfiction bestseller by an African-American woman. It was followed by six more autobiographies, several books of poetry, and essays. As a civil rights activist, she worked with Malcolm X and Dr. Martin Luther King, Jr.. Her *Georgia, Georgia* (1972) was the first feature film written by a black woman. As one of her husbands said, she accomplished more in a decade than many artists hope to achieve in a lifetime.

MATERIALS

B-1 or C-2 (2.5 mm) crochet hook

$5/16$" (8 mm) safety eyes

Tapestry needle

Polyester fiberfill

Black thread for embroidery

Small amount of white felt

Fabric for the head wrap: 4½ x 17½" (11.5 x 45 cm)

Thread matching the fabric

YARNS

Scheepjes Catona 100% cotton yarn:

507 Chocolate—skin, 25 g

263 Petal Peach—panties, 4 g

408 Old Rose—dress, 18 g

164 Light Navy—dress, bow, 6 g

110 Jet Black—hair, shoes, 6 g

074 Mercury—hair, 2 g

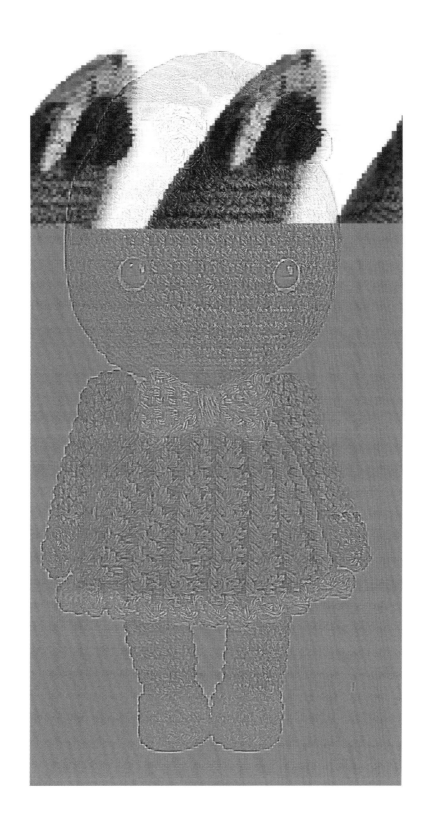

HEAD

Start with the skin color.

Rnd 1. 6 sc into magic ring (6).

Rnd 2. 2 sc into each (12).

Rnd 3. {sc, inc} 6 times (18).

Rnd 4. {sc into 2, inc} 6 times (24).

Rnd 5. {sc into 3, inc} 6 times (30).

Rnd 6. {sc into 4, inc} 6 times (36).

Rnd 7. {sc into 5, inc} 6 times (42).

Rnd 8. {sc into 6, inc} 6 times (48).

Rnd 9. {sc into 7, inc} 6 times (54).

Rnds 10–16. Sc into each (54).

Rnd 17. {sc into 8, inc} 6 times (60).

Rnds 18–20. Sc into each (60).

Rnd 21. {sc into 8, dec} 6 times (54).

Rnd 22. {sc into 7, dec} 6 times (48).

Rnd 23. {sc into 6, dec} 6 times (42).

Rnd 24. {sc into 5, dec} 6 times (36).

Add the eyes (see here for guidance).

Rnd 25. {sc into 4, dec} 6 times (30).

Rnd 26. {sc into 3, dec} 6 times (24).

Start to stuff the head.

Rnd 27. {sc into 2, dec} 6 times (18).

Rnd 28. {sc, dec} 6 times (12).

Continue to stuff the head firmly.

Rnd 29. Sc into each FLO (12).

Do not fasten off, continue with the body.

BODY

Rnd 1. BLO {sc into 2, inc} 4 times (16).

Rnd 2. {sc into 3, inc} 4 times (20).

Rnd 3. Sc into each (20).

Rnd 4. {sc into 4, inc} 4 times (24).

Rnd 5. Sc into each (24).

Rnd 6. {sc into 5, inc} 4 times (28).

Rnd 7. Sc into each (28).

Rnd 8. {sc into 6, inc} 4 times (32).

Rnd 9. {sc into 7, inc} 4 times (36).

Rnd 10. Sc into each (36).

Change to the color of the panties.

Rnds 11–12. Sc into each (36).

Rnd 13. {sc into 16, dec} 2 times (34).

Rnds 14–15. Sc into each (34).

Fasten off and weave in the ends. Stuff the neck and body continuously.

DRESS

Before continuing with the legs, crochet the dress.

Using the color of the dress, join with a sl st to a front loop of round 29 at the center back of the head. Work continuously, but join with a sl st at the end of each round. Ch 2 at the beginning does not count as dc.

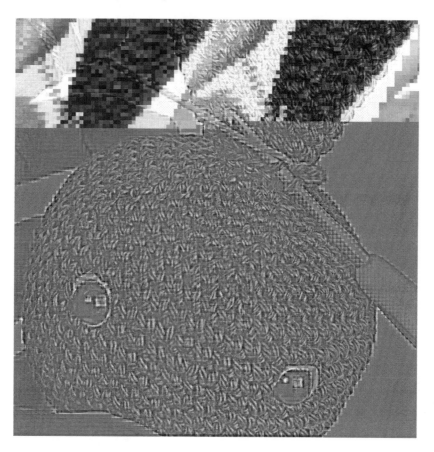

Rnd 1. {sc, inc} 6 times (18).

Rnd 2. Ch 2, 2 dc into each (36).

Rnd 3. Ch 2, {fpdc into next dc, bpdc into next dc} 18 times (36).

Rnds 4–5. Ch 2, {fpdc into prev rnd fpdc, bpdc into each of next 2 prev rnd bpdc} 18 times (36).

Rnd 6. Ch 2, {fpdc into prev rnd fpdc, 2 bpdc into prev rnd bpdc} 18 times (54).

Rnds 7–13. Ch 2, {fpdc into prev rnd fpdc, bpdc into each of next 2 prev rnd bpdc} 18 times (54).

Change to blue yarn.

Rnd 14. {(sc, dc, sc) into same st, sl st into next} 27 times. Fasten off and weave in the ends.

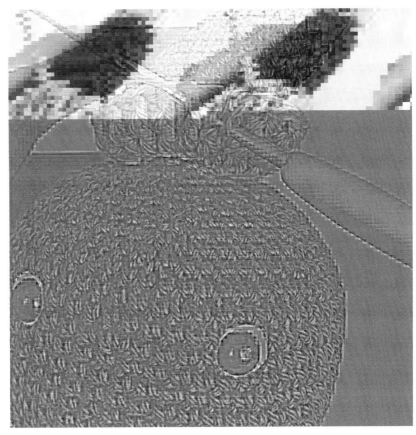

Round 3, Dress

LEGS

To make the legs, divide the work: 14 stitches for each of the legs, and 3 stitches between the legs, both front and back. Mark the stitches with yarn or a stitch marker. Make sure the legs line up with the eyes. Use skin-colored yarn and join with a sl st at the back of the doll to start.

Rnds 1–3. Sc into each (14).

Rnd 4. {sc into 5, dec} 2 times (12).

Rnds 5–8. Sc into each (12).

Stuff the body firmly and stuff the leg as you crochet it.

Rnd 9. {sc into 4, dec} 2 times (10).

Rnds 10–12. Sc into each (10). Stuff the legs firmly.

Rnd 13. Dec 5 times (5).

Fasten off, sew up the small hole, and weave in the ends. For the second leg, rejoin with a sl st at the back of the doll and work the leg. When finished, use the peach yarn to sew up the hole between the legs. Weave in the ends.

ARMS

Start with the color of the dress, make two.

Rnd 1. 6 sc into magic ring (6).

Rnd 2. Inc 6 times (12).

Rnds 3–4. Sc into each (12).

Rnd 5. {sc, dec} 4 times (8).

Stuff the upper part of the arm slightly.

Rnds 6–12. Sc into each (8).

Change to the skin color.

Rnd 13. Sc into each BLO (8).

Rnd 14. {sc into 3, inc} 2 times (10).

Rnd 15. Sc into each (10).

Rnd 16. Dec 5 times (5).

Fasten off and leave a long tail for sewing. Sew the hole closed and weave in the ends. Position an arm on each side of the doll and sew them into place.

BOW

Use the blue yarn.

Row 1. Ch 9, sc into 2nd ch from hook and into next 7 (8).

Rows 2–5. Ch 1, sc into each BLO (8).

Fasten off and leave a long tail for sewing. Thread the tail into a needle and insert it through the top loops of the last row until you reach the center. Wrap the tail over a few times to make a nice center and sew the bow onto the dress.

SHOES

Use the color for the shoes, make two.

Rnd 1. Ch 4, 2 sc into 2nd ch from hook, sc, 3 sc into next. Continue working on the other side of the foundation chain: sc, 2 sc into last (9).

Rnd 2. Inc 2 times, sc, inc 3 times, sc, inc 2 times (16).

Rnd 3. Sc into each BLO (16).

Rnd 4. Sc into 5, dec 3 times, sc into 5 (13).

Rnd 5. Sc into 6, dec, sc into 5 (12).

Fasten off and leave a long tail for sewing. Add stuffing to the toe of the shoes, position them on the legs, and sew them into place. Weave in the ends.

EYEBROWS AND NOSE

Using black thread, embroider the eyebrows between rounds 12 and 14. With skin-colored yarn, embroider the nose between rounds 18 and 19.

HAIR AND HEAD WRAP

Make three locks with black yarn and one with gray yarn. Ch 15, 2 sc into 2nd ch from hook and into each ch (28). Fasten off and leave long tail for sewing. Place the locks onto the head and sew them into place.

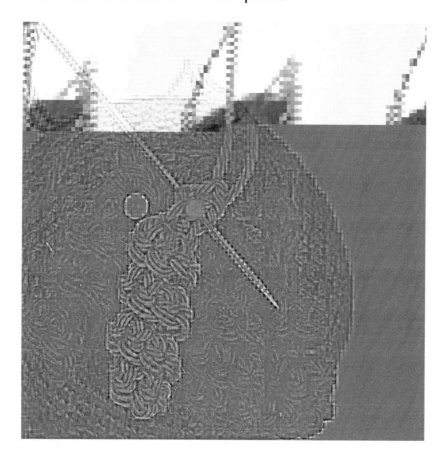

Place the doll's head into the middle of the fabric and tie a knot at the top of the head. Arrange the ends neatly, secure them with pins, and sew the ensemble onto the head with matching thread.

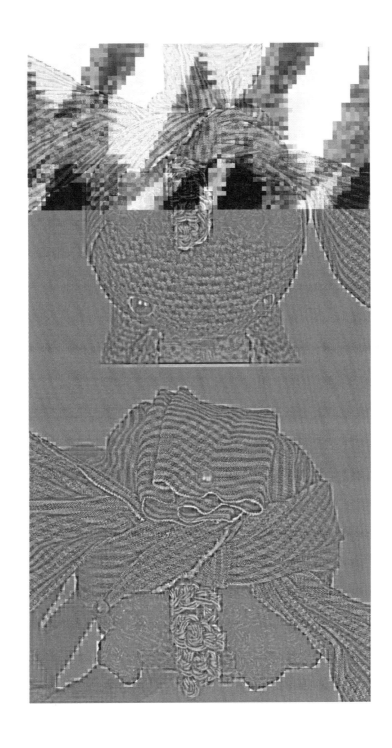

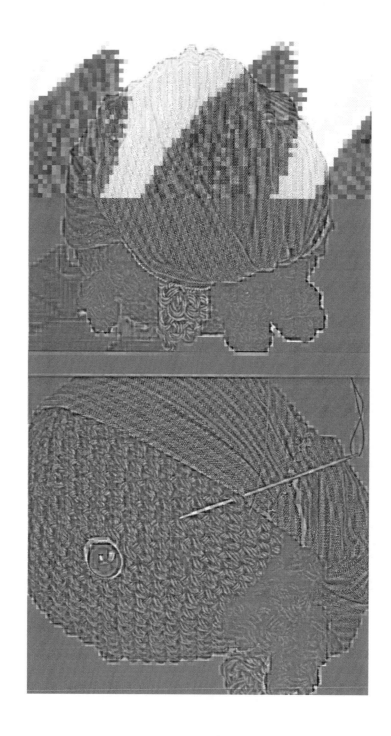

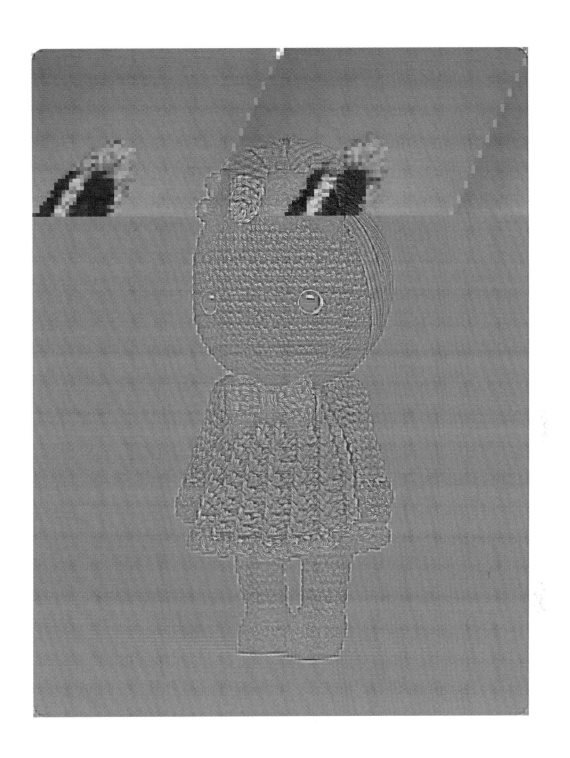

JANE AUSTEN

English novelist Jane Austen is world-renowned for her six major novels. As a young lady in eighteenth-century England, Jane was obsessed with books and was just eleven years old when she started to write poems and stories. Jane's timeless appeal is characterized by her humorous and satirical observations of eighteenth-century society. She was ahead of her time in the way she wrote about women, love, and marriage, and profoundly altered the sentimental narrative for girls—and we couldn't love her more for it!

MATERIALS

B-1 or C-2 (2.5 mm) crochet hook

$5/16$" (8 mm) safety eyes

Tapestry needle

Polyester fiberfill

Black thread for embroidery

Small amount of white felt

YARNS

Scheepjes Catona 100% cotton yarn:

130 Old Lace—skin, 22 g

528 Silver Blue—dress (A), 18 g

403 Lemonade—dress (B), panties, 7 g

502 Camel—shoes, 3 g

507 Chocolate—hair, 18 g

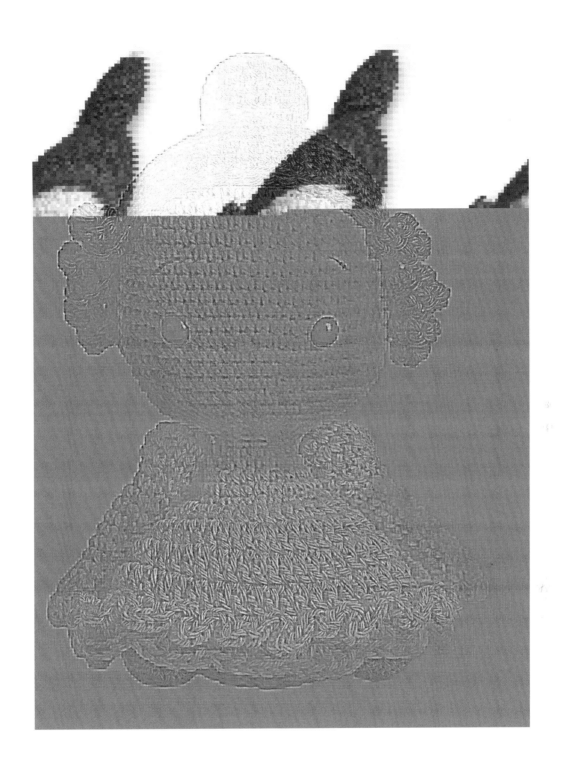

HEAD

Start with the skin color.

Rnd 1. 6 sc into magic ring (6).

Rnd 2. 2 sc into each (12).

Rnd 3. {sc, inc} 6 times (18).

Rnd 4. {sc into 2, inc} 6 times (24).

Rnd 5. {sc into 3, inc} 6 times (30).

Rnd 6. {sc into 4, inc} 6 times (36).

Rnd 7. {sc into 5, inc} 6 times (42).

Rnd 8. {sc into 6, inc} 6 times (48).

Rnd 9. {sc into 7, inc} 6 times (54).

Rnds 10–16. Sc into each (54).

Rnd 17. {sc into 8, inc} 6 times (60).

Rnds 18–20. Sc into each (60).

Rnd 21. {sc into 8, dec} 6 times (54).

Rnd 22. {sc into 7, dec} 6 times (48).

Rnd 23. {sc into 6, dec} 6 times (42).

Rnd 24. {sc into 5, dec} 6 times (36).

Add the eyes (see here for guidance).

Rnd 25. {sc into 4, dec} 6 times (30).

Rnd 26. {sc into 3, dec} 6 times (24).

Start to stuff the head.

Rnd 27. {sc into 2, dec} 6 times (18).

Rnd 28. {sc, dec} 6 times (12).

Continue to stuff the head firmly.

Rnd 29. Sc into each FLO (12).

Do not fasten off, continue with the body.

BODY

Rnd 1. {sc, inc} 6 times (18).

Rnd 2. {sc into 2, inc} 6 times (24). Change to the color of the dress.

Rnd 3. Sc into each (24).

Rnd 4. {sc into 3, inc} 6 times (30).

Rnd 5. Sc into each (30).

Change to the skin color.

Rnd 6. Sc into each BLO (30).

Rnd 7. {sc into 4, inc} 6 times (36).

Rnds 8–9. Sc into each (36).

Rnd 10. {sc into 5, inc} 6 times (42).

Rnds 11–12. Sc into each (42).

Stuff the neck and body continuously.

Change to the color of the panties.

Rnds 13–15. Sc into each (42).

Rnd 16. {sc into 5, dec} 6 times (36).

Rnd 17. Sc into each (36).

Rnd 18. {sc into 4, dec} 6 times (30).

Rnd 19. {sc into 3, dec} 6 times (24).

Rnd 20. {sc into 2, dec} 6 times (18).

Stuff the body firmly.

Rnd 21. {sc, dec} 6 times (12).

Rnd 22. Dec 6 times (6).

Fasten off and leave a long tail for sewing. Sew up the hole and weave in the ends.

DRESS

Using dress color A (silver blue), join with a sl st to a front loop of round 5 at the center back of the body. Work continuously, but join with a sl st at the end of each round. Start rounds 1 to 5 with ch 2, which does not count as dc. Start rounds 6 to 7 with ch 1, which does not count as sc.

Rnd 1. Ch 2, {dc, inc} 15 times (45).

Rnd 2. Ch 2, {dc into 2, inc} 15 times (60).

Rnds 3–5. Ch 2, dc into each (60).

Rnd 6. Ch 1, FLO 3 hdc into each (180).

Fasten off and weave in the ends.

Rnd 7. With dress color B (yellow), join with a sl st into a back loop of round 5. Ch 1, BLO {sc, sk 1 st, 5 dc into next, sk 1 st} 15 times (15 shells).

Fasten off and weave in the ends.

EYEBROWS AND NOSE

Using black thread, embroider the eyebrows between rounds 12 and 14. With skin-colored yarn, embroider the nose between rounds 18 and 19. You can add a cheek blush with makeup or watercolor pencil.

HAIR

Use the hair color.

Rnd 1. 6 sc into magic ring (6).

Rnd 2. 2 sc into each (12).

Rnd 3. {sc, inc} 6 times (18).

Rnd 4. {sc into 2, inc} 6 times (24).

Rnd 5. {sc into 3, inc} 6 times (30).

Rnd 6. {sc into 4, inc} 6 times (36).

Rnd 7. {sc into 5, inc} 6 times (42).

Rnd 8. {sc into 6, inc} 6 times (48).

Rnd 9. {sc into 7, inc} 6 times (54).

Rnds 10–18. Sc into each (54). Do not fasten off, sl st into next st.

Curl 1. Ch 8, 2 sc into 2nd ch from hook and next 6, sl st into next 3 on the hair.

Curl 2. Repeat curl 1.

Curl 3. Ch 8, 2 sc into 2nd ch from hook and next 6, sl st into next 18 on the hair.

Curls 4–6. Repeat curl 1.

Fasten off and leave a long tail for sewing. Place the hair on the head, secure it with pins, and sew it into place.

BUN

Use the hair color.

Rnd 1. 6 sc into magic ring (6).

Rnd 2. 2 sc into each (12).

Rnd 3. {sc, inc} 6 times (18).

Rnd 4. {sc into 2, inc} 6 times (24).

Rnds 5–6. Sc into each (24).

Rnd 7. {sc into 2, dec} 6 times (18).

Rnd 8. {sc, dec} 6 times (12).

Fasten off and leave a long tail for sewing. Stuff the bun, then place it on the head between rounds 1 and 6 of the hair. Secure the bun with pins, and sew it into place.

ARMS

Start with the color of the dress, make two.

Rnd 1. 6 sc into magic ring (6).

Rnd 2. 2 sc into each (12).

Rnd 3. {sc, inc} 6 times (18).

Rnd 4. Sc into each (18).

Rnd 5. {sc, dec} 6 times (12).

Rnd 6. {sc, dec} 4 times (8).

Slightly stuff the dress part of the arms.

Change to the skin color.

Rnds 7–14. Sc into each (8).

Rnd 15. {sc into 2, inc} 2 times, sc into last 2 (10).

Rnd 16. Sc into each (10).

Rnd 17. Dec 5 times (5).

Fasten off and leave a long tail for sewing. Sew up the hole and weave in the ends.

LEGS

Start with the skin color, make two.

Rnd 1. 6 sc into magic ring (6).

Rnd 2. 2 sc into each (12).

Rnd 3. {sc into 2, inc} 4 times (16).

Rnds 4–5. Sc into each (16).

Rnd 6. {sc into 2, dec} 4 times (12).

Rnds 7–12. Sc into each (12).

Rnd 13. Inc 2 times, sc into 10 (14).

Change to the color of the shoes.

Rnd 14. Inc 4 times, sc into 10 (18).

Rnds 15–16. Sc into each (18).

Rnd 17. Dec 9 times (9).

Start to stuff the leg.

Rnd 18. Dec 3 more times.

Stuff the toe of the leg. Fasten off and leave a long tail for sewing. Sew up the hole and weave in the ends. Position an arm and leg on each side of the doll and sew them into place.

BRUCE LEE

American-born Bruce Lee was a movie star, a cultural icon, and the most influential martial artist of the twentieth century. Alongside his lifelong dedication to practicing martial arts, Lee studied dramatic arts, philosophy, and psychology at college. He founded a martial arts academy to pass on what he had learned to students. Lee soon came to the attention of a Hollywood producer and quickly became a superstar. His four most legendary movies—*Fist of Fury, Enter the Dragon, The Way of the Dragon*, and *The Game of Death*—have been watched by millions and have made him a movie icon.

MATERIALS

B-1 or C-2 (2.5 mm) crochet hook

$5/16$" (8 mm) oval safety eyes

Tapestry needle

Polyester fiberfill

Black thread for embroidery

YARNS

Scheepjes Catona 100% cotton yarn:

505 Linen—skin, 20 g

522 Primrose—jumpsuit, 22 g

110 Jet Black—hair, shoes, stripes, 18 g

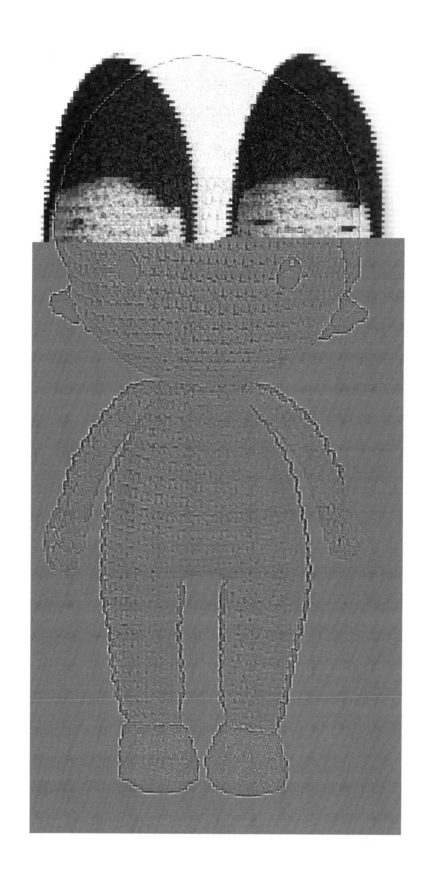

HEAD

Start with the skin color.

Rnd 1. 6 sc into magic ring (6).

Rnd 2. 2 sc into each (12).

Rnd 3. {sc, inc} 6 times (18).

Rnd 4. {sc into 2, inc} 6 times (24).

Rnd 5. {sc into 3, inc} 6 times (30).

Rnd 6. {sc into 4, inc} 6 times (36).

Rnd 7. {sc into 5, inc} 6 times (42).

Rnd 8. {sc into 6, inc} 6 times (48).

Rnd 9. {sc into 7, inc} 6 times (54).

Rnds 10–16. Sc into each (54).

Rnd 17. {sc into 8, inc} 6 times (60).

Rnds 18–20. Sc into each (60).

Rnd 21. {sc into 8, dec} 6 times (54).

Rnd 22. {sc into 7, dec} 6 times (48).

Rnd 23. {sc into 6, dec} 6 times (42).

Rnd 24. {sc into 5, dec} 6 times (36).

Add the eyes (see here for guidance). Before placing them, use black thread to embroider two long horizontal stitches from the eye position outward.

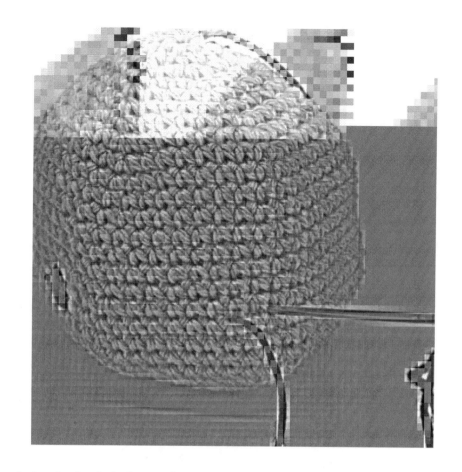

Rnd 25. {sc into 4, dec} 6 times (30).

Rnd 26. {sc into 3, dec} 6 times (24). Start to stuff the head.

Rnd 27. {sc into 2, dec} 6 times (18).

Rnd 28. {sc, dec} 6 times (12). Continue to stuff the head firmly.

Rnd 29. Sc into each FLO (12). Change to the color of the jumpsuit.

BODY

From round 2 crochet into BLO throughout the jumpsuit.

Rnd 1. {sc, inc} 6 times (18).

Rnd 2. BLO {sc into 2, inc} 6 times (24).

Rnd 3. BLO sc into each (24).

Rnd 4. BLO {sc into 3, inc} 6 times (30).

Rnd 5. BLO sc into each (30).

Rnd 6. BLO {sc into 4, inc} 6 times (36).

Rnds 7–12. BLO sc into each (36).

Rnd 13. BLO {sc into 16, dec} 2 times (34).

Rnd 14. BLO sc into each (34).

Do not fasten off, continue with the legs. Stuff the neck and body continuously.

LEGS

To make the legs, divide the work: 14 stitches for each of the legs, and 3 stitches between the legs, both front and back. Mark the stitches with yarn or a stitch marker. Make sure the legs line up with the eyes. If the last stitch of the body is within the 14 stitches for the legs, then continue crocheting. If it is within the 3 stitches, then fasten off, leave a tail for sewing later, and rejoin the jumpsuit-colored yarn with a sl st at the back of the doll.

Rnds 1–3. BLO sc into each (14).

Rnd 4. BLO {sc into 5, dec} 2 times (12).

Rnds 5–8. BLO sc into each (12).

Stuff the body firmly and stuff the leg as you crochet it.

Rnd 9. BLO {sc into 4, dec} 2 times (10).

Rnd 10. BLO sc into each (10).

Change to the skin color.

Rnd 11. BLO sc into each (10).

Rnd 12. Sc into each (10).

Stuff the leg firmly.

Rnd 13. Dec 5 times (5).

Fasten off, sew up the small hole, and weave in the ends. For the second leg, rejoin with a sl st at the back of the doll and work the leg. When finished, sew up the hole between the legs. Weave in the ends.

EYEBROWS AND NOSE

Using black thread, embroider the eyebrows between rounds 14 and 15, right above the eyes. With skin-colored yarn, embroider the nose between rounds 18 and 19.

JUMPSUIT EMBROIDERY

Using black yarn, pull the needle through between rounds 10 and 11 on the outside of the jumpsuit leg and then thread it through each front loop, working upward in a straight line until you reach the first round of the jumpsuit. Then, working downward, pull the needle from right to left through each black stitch between the front loops, all the way down. Fasten off and weave in the ends. Repeat on the other side of the doll and on the insides of the legs.

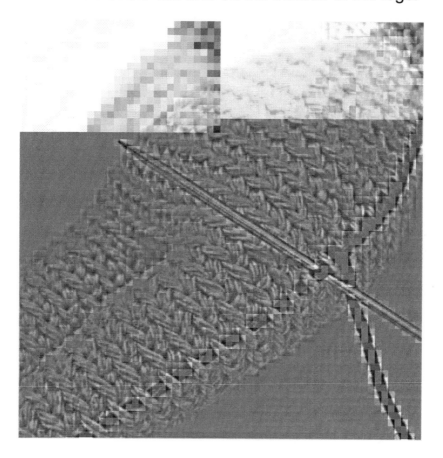

ARMS

Start with the skin color, make two.

Rnd 1. 6 sc into magic ring (6).

Rnd 2. {sc, inc} 3 times (9).

Rnd 3. Sc into each (9).

Rnd 4. {sc into 2, dec} 2 times, sc into last (7).

Change to the color of the jumpsuit.

Rnd 5. Sc into each (7).

Rnds 6–13. Sc into each BLO.

Fasten off and leave a long tail for sewing. Embroider the black lines on the outside of both arms using the same method as for the stripes on the legs. Use small stitches to sew the arms onto the body.

SHOES

Use the color of the shoes, make two.

Rnd 1. Ch 4, 2 sc into 2nd ch from hook, sc, 3 sc into next. Continue working on the other side of the foundation chain: sc, 2 sc into last (9).

Rnd 2. Inc 2 times, sc, inc 3 times, sc, inc 2 times (16).

Rnd 3. Sc into each BLO (16).

Rnd 4. Sc into 5, dec 3 times, sc into 5 (13).

Rnd 5. Sc into 5, dec, sc into 6 (12).

Fasten off and leave a long tail for sewing. Add stuffing to the toe of the shoes, position them on the legs, and sew them into place. Weave in the ends.

HAIR

Use the hair color.

Rnd 1. 6 sc into magic ring (6).

Rnd 2. 2 sc into each (12).

Rnd 3. {sc, inc} 6 times (18).

Rnd 4. {sc into 2, inc} 6 times (24).

Rnd 5. {sc into 3, inc} 6 times (30).

Rnd 6. {sc into 4, inc} 6 times (36).

Rnd 7. {sc into 5, inc} 6 times (42).

Rnd 8. {sc into 6, inc} 6 times (48).

Rnd 9. {sc into 7, inc} 6 times (54).

Rnds 10–17. Sc into each (54).

Rnd 18. Sc into next, hdc into next, dc into next 4, hdc into next, sc into next 4, sl st into next, * ch 3, sl st into 2nd ch from hook and into next, sl st into next on the wig. Repeat from * 11 times. Sc into next 4, hdc into next, dc into next 4, hdc into next, sc into next 2, sl st into next, ** ch 4, sl st into 2nd ch from hook and into next 2, sl st into next on the wig. Repeat from ** 16 times. Sc into last.

Fasten off and leave a long tail for sewing. Place the hair on the head, secure it with pins, and sew it into place.

JACKIE ROBINSON

American baseball player Jackie Robinson fought for equal rights all his life; he was a pioneer, a fighter, and an amazing athlete. Robinson was the first player to break Major League Baseball's color barrier, ending the segregation that had been present in MLB for more than fifty years. Robinson played for the Brooklyn Dodgers and won the Rookie of the Year Award in 1947, establishing himself as one of the best players in the league. Later he was inducted into the Baseball Hall of Fame. They say that behind every successful man there is a woman, and, in Robinson's case, this woman was Rachel Isum, who became his wife in 1946. She and their three children provided Jackie with the emotional support he needed during his fight for equal rights.

MATERIALS

B-1 or C-2 (2.5 mm) crochet hook

$5/16$" (8 mm) safety eyes

Tapestry needle

Polyester fiberfill

Black thread for embroidery

Small amount of white felt

YARNS

Scheepjes Catona 100% cotton yarn:

507 Chocolate—skin, 20 g

106 Snow White—shirt, shorts, 20 g

247 Bluebird—hat, undershirt, 18 g

110 Jet Black—hair, shoes, 18 g

074 Mercury—socks, 12 g

115 Hot Red—jersey number, 1 g

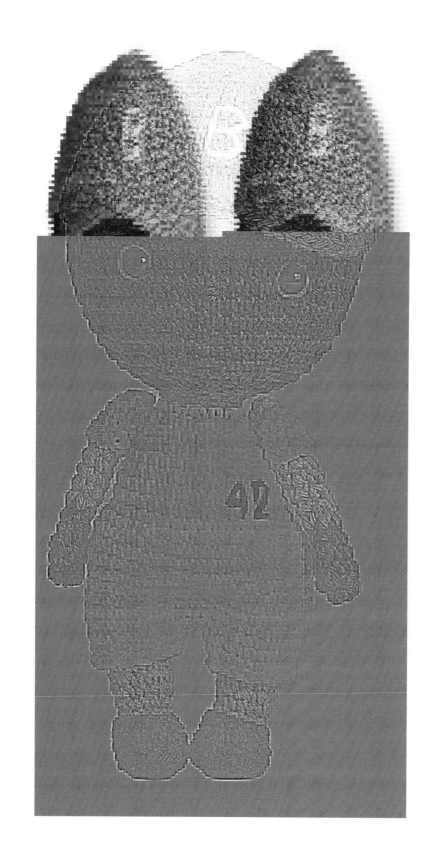

HEAD

Start with the skin color.

Rnd 1. 6 sc into magic ring (6).

Rnd 2. 2 sc into each (12).

Rnd 3. {sc, inc} 6 times (18).

Rnd 4. {sc into 2, inc} 6 times (24).

Rnd 5. {sc into 3, inc} 6 times (30).

Rnd 6. {sc into 4, inc} 6 times (36).

Rnd 7. {sc into 5, inc} 6 times (42).

Rnd 8. {sc into 6, inc} 6 times (48).

Rnd 9. {sc into 7, inc} 6 times (54).

Rnds 10–16. Sc into each (54).

Rnd 17. {sc into 8, inc} 6 times (60).

Rnds 18–20. Sc into each (60).

Rnd 21. {sc into 8, dec} 6 times (54).

Rnd 22. {sc into 7, dec} 6 times (48).

Rnd 23. {sc into 6, dec} 6 times (42).

Rnd 24. {sc into 5, dec} 6 times (36).

Add the eyes (see here for guidance).

Rnd 25. {sc into 4, dec} 6 times (30).

Rnd 26. {sc into 3, dec} 6 times (24).

Start to stuff the head.

Rnd 27. {sc into 2, dec} 6 times (18).

Rnd 28. {sc, dec} 6 times (12).

Continue to stuff the head firmly.

Rnd 29. Sc into each FLO (12).

Change to the white shirt yarn.

BODY

Rnd 1. {sc, inc} 6 times (18).

Rnd 2. {sc into 2, inc} 6 times (24).

Rnd 3. Sc into each (24).

Rnd 4. {sc into 3, inc} 6 times (30).

Rnd 5. Sc into each (30).

Rnds 6. {sc into 4, inc} 6 times (36).

Rnds 7–8. Sc into each (36).

Rnd 9. Sc into each (36).

Change to the color of the socks.

Rnd 10. Sc into each BLO (36).

Rnds 11–12. Sc into each (36).

Rnd 13. {sc into 16, dec} 2 times (34).

Rnds 14–15. Sc into each (34).

Do not fasten off, continue with the legs. Stuff the neck and body continuously.

LEGS

To make the legs, divide the work: 14 stitches for each of the legs, and 3 stitches between the legs, both front and back. Mark the stitches with yarn or a stitch marker. Make sure the legs line up with the eyes. If the last stitch of the body is within the 14 stitches for the legs, then continue crocheting. If it is within the 3 stitches, then fasten off, leave a tail for sewing later, and rejoin the sock-colored yarn with a sl st at the back of the doll.

Rnds 1–3. Sc into each (14).

Rnd 4. {sc into 5, dec} 2 times (12).

Rnds 5–8. Sc into each (12).

Stuff the body firmly and stuff the leg as you crochet it.

Rnd 9. {sc into 4, dec} 2 times (10).

Rnds 10–12. Sc into each (10).

Stuff the leg firmly.

Rnd 13. Dec 5 times (5).

Fasten off, sew up the small hole, and weave in the ends. For the second leg, rejoin with a sl st at the back of the doll and work the leg. When finished, sew up the hole between the legs. Weave in the ends.

EYEBROWS AND NOSE

Using black thread, embroider the eyebrows between rounds 12 and 14. With skin-colored yarn, embroider the nose between rounds 18 and 19.

SHORTS

Using the color of the shorts, join with a sl st to a front loop of round 9 at the center back of the body. Work continuously but join with a sl st at the end of each round. Ch 1 at the beginning does not count as sc.

Rnd 1. Ch 1, {sc, inc} 18 times. (54).

Rnds 2–4. Ch 1, sc into each. (54).

Rnd 5. Ch 1, {sc into 4, dec} 9 times. (45).

Rnds 6–8. Ch 1, sc into each. (45).

Rnd 9. Ch 1, dec, sc into each. (44).

Do not fasten off. Divide the piece into two sections of 22 stitches to form the legs of the shorts. Make sure to align the middle of the shorts with the doll's legs, nose, and eyes. Now work each shorts leg continuously but without joining each round with a sl st.

SHORTS LEGS

Rnd 1. Sc into each (22).

Rnd 2. {sc into 5, dec} 3 times, sc into last (19).

Rnd 3. Sc into each (19).

Rnd 4. Sl st into each (19).

Fasten off and weave in the ends. Rejoin to the shorts at the back of the doll for the other shorts leg and repeat rounds 1–4. Fasten off and weave in the ends.

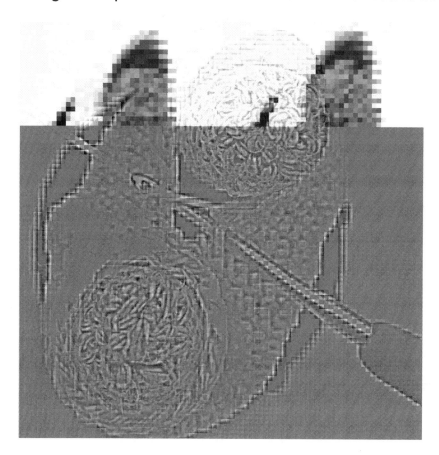

ARMS

Start with the skin color, make two.

Rnd 1. 6 sc into magic ring (6).

Rnd 2. {sc, inc} 3 times (9).

Rnd 3. Sc into each (9).

Rnd 4. {sc into 2, dec} 2 times, sc into last (7).

Rnd 5. Sc into each (7).

Change to the blue undershirt yarn.

Rnds 6–13. Sc into each.

Fasten off and sew the hole closed. Weave in the ends.

SHIRT SLEEVES

Use the white shirt yarn, make two.

Rnd 1. 6 sc into magic ring (6).

Rnd 2. {sc, inc} 3 times (9).

Rnds 3–5. Sc into each (9).

Fasten off and leave a long tail for sewing. Place the arms into the sleeves. Using small stitches, sew the sleeves onto the arms. Sew the sleeved arms onto the body.

SHOES

Use the color of the shoes, make two.

Rnd 1. Ch 4, 2 sc into 2nd ch from hook, sc, 3 sc into next. Continue working on the other side of the foundation chain: sc, 2 sc into last (9).

Rnd 2. Inc 2 times, sc, inc 3 times, sc, inc 2 times (16).

Rnd 3. Sc into each BLO (16).

Rnd 4. Sc into 5, dec 3 times, sc into 5 (13).

Rnd 5. Sc into 6, dec, sc into 5 (12).

Fasten off and leave a long tail for sewing. Add stuffing to the toe of the shoes, position them on the legs, and sew them into place. Weave in the ends.

HAIR

Use the hair color.

Rnd 1. 6 sc into magic ring (6).

Rnd 2. 2 sc into each (12).

Rnd 3. {sc, inc} 6 times (18).

Rnd 4. {sc into 2, inc} 6 times (24).

Rnd 5. {sc into 3, inc} 6 times (30).

Rnd 6. {sc into 4, inc} 6 times (36).

Rnd 7. {sc into 5, inc} 6 times (42).

Rnd 8. {sc into 6, inc} 6 times (48).

Rnd 9. {sc into 7, inc} 6 times (54).

Rnds 10–17. Sc into each (54).

Rnd 18. Sc into 16, hdc into next 4, sl st into next 2, hdc into next 2, dc into next 6, hdc into next 2, sl st into next 2, hdc into next 4, sc into next 16.

Rnd 19. Sc into 6, sl st into next.

Fasten off and leave a long tail for sewing. Place the hair on the head, secure it with pins, and sew it into place.

HAT

Use the color of the hat.

Work each sc in an "X" shape (see here) until the hat is complete, or use standard sc if you prefer.

Rnd 1. 6 sc into magic ring (6).

Rnd 2. 2 sc into each (12).

Rnd 3. {sc, inc} 6 times (18).

Rnd 4. {sc into 2, inc} 6 times (24).

Rnd 5. {sc into 3, inc} 6 times (30).

Rnd 6. {sc into 4, inc} 6 times (36).

Rnd 7. {sc into 5, inc} 6 times (42).

Rnd 8. {sc into 6, inc} 6 times (48).

Rnd 9. {sc into 7, inc} 6 times (54).

Rnd 10. {sc into 8, inc} 6 times (60).

Rnds 11–19. Sc into each (60).

Continue crocheting the brim. Work in rows, turning at the end of each row. Ch 1 at the beginning does not count as sc.

Row 20. Ch 1, FLO {sc into 2, inc} 6 times, turn (24).

Row 21. Ch 1, sk first stitch, sc into next 21, dec, turn (22).

Row 22. Ch 1, sk first stitch, sc into next 19, dec, turn (20).

Row 23. Ch 1, sk first stitch, sc into next 17, dec, turn (18).

Row 24. Ch 1, sk first stitch, sc into next 15, dec (16).

Do not fasten off, crochet around the hat. Sc into the same stitch, then crochet evenly along the side of the brim (about 4 sc), then sc into each st around the hat, crochet 4 sc along the other side of the brim, and join with a sl st to the first sc of row 24. Fasten off and weave in the ends.

CLOTHING EMBROIDERY

Using white yarn, embroider a letter "B" on the center front of the hat between rounds 13 and 18. Use pins as a guide to help you form the letter. Then, insert the needle behind each white stitch all the way around to produce a thicker white line. Last, embroider the line across the middle of the letter.

Using red yarn, embroider the number 42 onto the left side of the shirt between rounds 6 and 9 of the body.

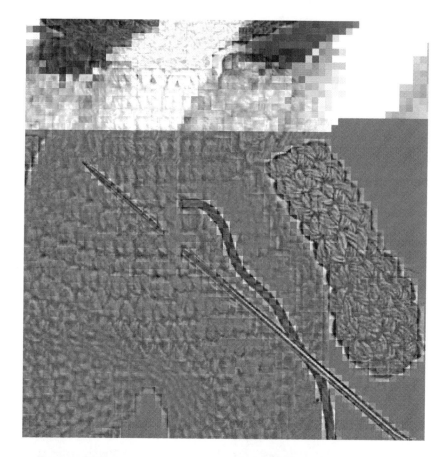

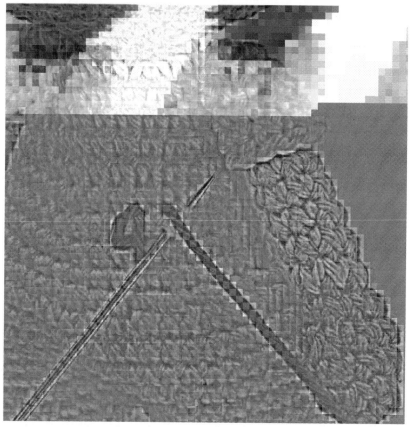

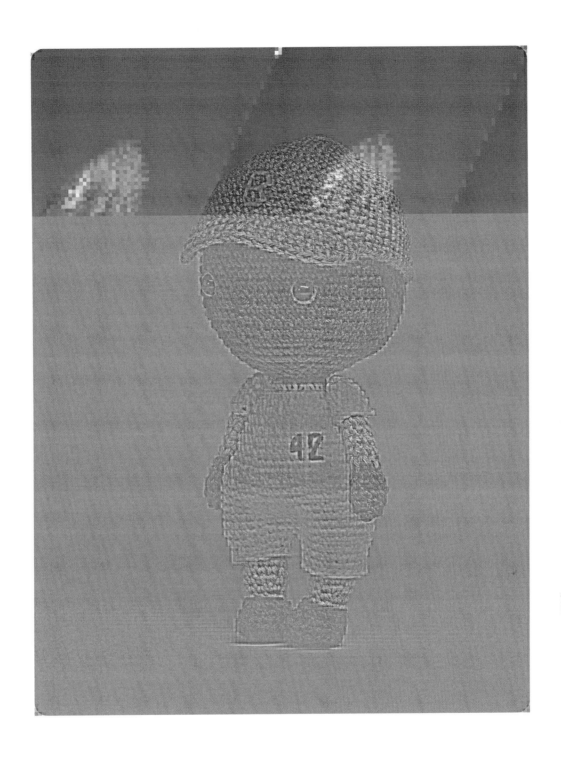

JANE GOODALL

Jane Goodall is an English anthropologist and primatologist. She is best known for studying the social and family life of chimpanzees. By immersing herself in the habitat of the chimps, she developed a close bond with them. She also gave them names instead of numbers, which was not common practice at the time. During her most famous study of chimpanzees—in Gombe, Tanzania, in the 1960s—Jane discovered that chimps experience emotions like joy and sorrow, and that they form long-term bonds. She also discovered that they make and use tools—a groundbreaking discovery. Jane was just twenty-six years old at that time, and she has subsequently spent more than sixty years protecting chimpanzees and their habitats.

MATERIALS

B-1 or C-2 (2.5 mm) crochet hook

$5/16$" (8 mm) safety eyes

Tapestry needle

Polyester fiberfill

Black thread for embroidery

Small amount of white felt

YARNS

Scheepjes Catona 100% cotton yarn:

130 Old Lace—skin, 20 g

502 Camel—shirt, 7 g

506 Caramel—shorts, 7 g

162 Black Coffee—boots, belt, 5 g

522 Primrose—hair, 18 g

HEAD

Start with the skin color.

Rnd 1. 6 sc into magic ring (6).

Rnd 2. 2 sc into each (12).

Rnd 3. {sc, inc} 6 times (18).

Rnd 4. {sc into 2, inc} 6 times (24).

Rnd 5. {sc into 3, inc} 6 times (30).

Rnd 6. {sc into 4, inc} 6 times (36).

Rnd 7. {sc into 5, inc} 6 times (42).

Rnd 8. {sc into 6, inc} 6 times (48).

Rnd 9. {sc into 7, inc} 6 times (54).

Rnds 10–16. Sc into each (54).

Rnd 17. {sc into 8, inc} 6 times (60).

Rnds 18–20. Sc into each (60).

Rnd 21. {sc into 8, dec} 6 times (54).

Rnd 22. {sc into 7, dec} 6 times (48).

Rnd 23. {sc into 6, dec} 6 times (42).

Rnd 24. {sc into 5, dec} 6 times (36).

Add the eyes (see here for guidance).

Rnd 25. {sc into 4, dec} 6 times (30).

Rnd 26. {sc into 3, dec} 6 times (24).

Start to stuff the head.

Rnd 27. {sc into 2, dec} 6 times (18).

Rnd 28. {sc, dec} 6 times (12).

Continue to stuff the head firmly.

Rnd 29. Sc into each FLO (12).

Change to the color of the shirt.

BODY

Rnd 1. {sc, inc} 6 times (18).

Rnd 2. {sc into 2, inc} 6 times (24).

Rnd 3. Sc into each (24).

Rnd 4. {sc into 3, inc} 6 times (30).

Rnd 5. Sc into each (30).

Rnd 6. {sc into 4, inc} 6 times (36).

Rnd 7. Sc into each (36).

Rnd 8. {sc into 5, inc} 6 times (42).

Rnd 9. Sc into each (42).

Rnd 10. Sc into each (42).

Change to the color of the belt.

Rnd 11. Hdc into each (42).

Change to the color of the shorts.

Rnds 12–15. Sc into each (42).

Rnd 16. {sc into 5, dec} 6 times (36).

Rnd 17. {sc into 4, dec} 6 times (30).

Rnd 18. {sc into 3, dec} 6 times (24).

Rnd 19. {sc into 2, dec} 6 times (18).

Stuff the body firmly.

Rnd 20. {sc, dec} 6 times (12).

Rnd 21. Dec 6 times (6).

Fasten off and leave a long tail for sewing. Sew up the hole and weave in the ends.

EYEBROWS AND NOSE

Using black thread, embroider the eyebrows between rounds 12 and 14. With skin-colored yarn, embroider the nose between rounds 18 and 19. You can add a cheek blush with makeup or watercolor pencil.

CLOTHING EMBROIDERY

Using the color of the shorts, embroider the collar and a straight line onto the shirt. Start by pulling the needle through between round 29 of the head and round 1 of the body. Embroider a straight line by pushing the needle into the body right above the belt. Make sure the line aligns with the nose. Pull the needle through between rounds 2 and 3 of the body, two stitches away from the line you just embroidered. Push the needle into the starting point and pull through at the center back of the doll. Finish one side of the collar by pushing the needle into the same stitch where you pulled through between rounds 2 and 3. Pull through between the same rounds on the other side of the line, two stitches away. Finish the other side of the collar in the same way. Weave in the ends. Using the skin-colored yarn, embroider a rectangle onto the belt. Fasten off and weave in the ends.

HAIR

Use the hair color.

Rnd 1. 6 sc into magic ring (6).

Rnd 2. 2 sc into each (12).

Rnd 3. {sc, inc} 6 times (18).

Rnd 4. {sc into 2, inc} 6 times (24).

Rnd 5. {sc into 3, inc} 6 times (30).

Rnd 6. {sc into 4, inc} 6 times (36).

Rnd 7. {sc into 5, inc} 6 times (42).

Rnd 8. {sc into 6, inc} 6 times (48).

Rnd 9. {sc into 7, inc} 6 times (54).

Rnds 10–17. Sc into each (54).

Rnd 18. Dc into next 25, hdc into next, sl st into next 2, hdc into next, dc into last 25 (54).

Fasten off and leave a long tail for sewing.

PONYTAIL

Using the hair color, ch 20, sl st into 2nd ch from hook and into each ch. Join this strand to the hair with a sl st between rounds 13 and 14, right above where you fastened off the hair. * Ch 20, sl st into 2nd ch from hook and into each ch. Join to the hair with a sl st next to the previous strand. Repeat from * 4 times. Fasten off and weave in the ends. Place the hair on the head, secure it with pins, and sew it into place. Using the color of the shorts, wind some yarn around the ponytail a few times, close to the hair. Weave in the ends.

ARMS

Use the skin color, make two.

Rnd 1. 6 sc into magic ring (6).

Rnd 2. {sc, inc} 3 times (9).

Rnd 3. Sc into each (9).

Rnd 4. {sc into 2, dec} 2 times, sc into last (7).

Rnds 5–13. Sc into each (7).

Fasten off and sew the hole closed. Weave in the ends.

SHIRT SLEEVES

Use the color of the shirt, make two.

Rnd 1. 6 sc into magic ring (6).

Rnd 2. {sc, inc} 3 times (9).

Rnds 3–5. Sc into each (9).

Fasten off and leave a long tail for sewing. Place the arms into the sleeves. Using small stitches, sew the sleeves onto the arms. Sew the sleeved arms onto the body.

LEGS

Start with the skin color, make two.

Rnd 1. 6 sc into magic ring (6).

Rnd 2. {sc, inc} 3 times (9).

Rnd 3. {sc into 2, inc} 3 times (12).

Rnds 4–10. Sc into each (12).

Change to the color of the boots.

Rnd 11. Sc into each (12).

Rnd 12. Inc 2 times, sc into 10 (14).

Rnd 13. Inc 4 times, sc into 10 (18).

Rnds 14–15. Sc into each (18).

Rnd 16. BLO dec 9 times (9).

Stuff the leg firmly.

Rnd 17. Dec 3 more times.

Stuff the toe of each leg. Fasten off and leave a long tail for sewing. Sew up the hole and weave in the ends.

SHORTS LEGS

Use the color of the shorts, make two.

Rnd 1. 6 sc into magic ring (6).

Rnd 2. Inc 6 times (12).

Rnd 3. {sc into 2, inc} 4 times (16).

Rnds 4–6. Sc into each (16).

Rnd 7. Sc into 3, sl st into 13 (16).

Rnd 8. Sl st into first 3.

Fasten off and leave a long tail for sewing. Place the legs into the shorts legs and sew the shorts onto the legs. Sew the finished legs onto the body continuously from the shorts legs to the boots.

MALALA YOUSAFZAI

Malala Yousafzai is a Pakistan-born activist and human rights advocate. She was just eleven years old when the Taliban took control of the town where she lived and banned girls from attending school. She spoke out about girls' rights to an education and became recognized for her activism. In 2012, a Taliban gunman shot her as she rode home on a bus. She woke up ten days later in a hospital in the UK. After several months of rehabilitation, she recovered and continued to fight for education and equality for girls. She founded the nonprofit organization Malala Fund with her father to fight for every girl's right to an education. At the age of seventeen, she was the corecipient of the 2014 Nobel Peace Prize for her work, and she became the youngest Nobel laureate.

MATERIALS

B-1 or C-2 (2.5 mm) crochet hook

$5/16$" (8 mm) safety eyes

Tapestry needle

Polyester fiberfill

Black thread for embroidery

Small amount of white felt

YARNS

Scheepjes Catona 100% cotton yarn:

502 Camel—skin, 20 g

391 Deep Ocean Green—shirt, 8 g

074 Mercury—pants, 10 g

162 Black Coffee—shoes, 3 g

110 Jet Black—hair, 18 g

517 Ruby—headscarf, 22 g

383 Ginger Gold—headscarf, 4 g

408 Old Rose—embroidery, 1 g

403 Lemonade—embroidery, 1 g

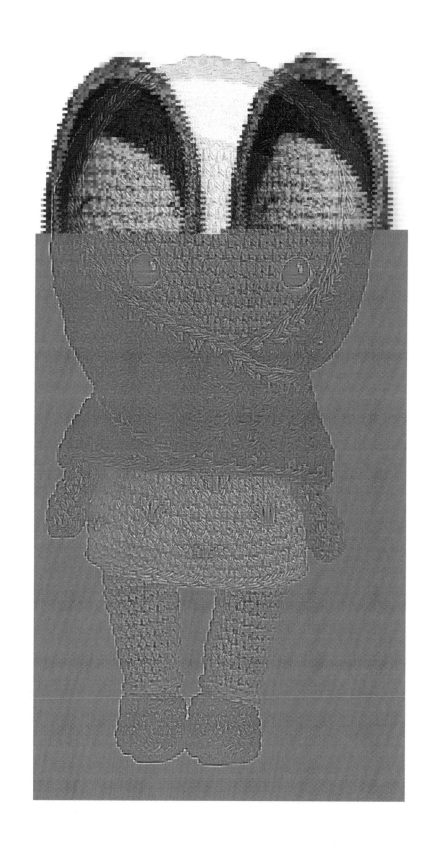

HEAD

Start with the skin color.

Rnd 1. 6 sc into magic ring (6).

Rnd 2. 2 sc into each (12).

Rnd 3. {sc, inc} 6 times (18).

Rnd 4. {sc into 2, inc} 6 times (24).

Rnd 5. {sc into 3, inc} 6 times (30).

Rnd 6. {sc into 4, inc} 6 times (36).

Rnd 7. {sc into 5, inc} 6 times (42).

Rnd 8. {sc into 6, inc} 6 times (48).

Rnd 9. {sc into 7, inc} 6 times (54).

Rnds 10–16. Sc into each (54).

Rnd 17. {sc into 8, inc} 6 times (60).

Rnds 18–20. Sc into each (60).

Rnd 21. {sc into 8, dec} 6 times (54).

Rnd 22. {sc into 7, dec} 6 times (48).

Rnd 23. {sc into 6, dec} 6 times (42).

Rnd 24. {sc into 5, dec} 6 times (36).

Add the eyes (see here for guidance).

Rnd 25. {sc into 4, dec} 6 times (30).

Rnd 26. {sc into 3, dec} 6 times (24).

Start to stuff the head.

Rnd 27. {sc into 2, dec} 6 times (18).

Rnd 28. {sc, dec} 6 times (12).

Continue to stuff the head firmly.

Rnd 29. Sc into each FLO (12).

Change to the color of the shirt.

BODY

Rnd 1. {sc, inc} 6 times (18).

Rnd 2. {sc into 2, inc} 6 times (24).

Rnd 3. Sc into each (24).

Rnd 4. {sc into 3, inc} 6 times (30).

Rnd 5. Sc into each (30).

Rnd 6. {sc into 4, inc} 6 times (36).

Rnds 7–9. Sc into each (36).

Rnd 10. Sc into each BLO (36).

Change to the color of the pants.

Rnds 11–12. Sc into each (36).

Rnd 13. {sc into 16, dec} 2 times (34).

Rnds 14–15. Sc into each (34).

Do not fasten off, continue with the legs. Stuff the neck and body continuously.

LEGS

To make the legs, divide the work: 14 stitches for each of the legs, and 3 stitches between the legs, both front and back. Mark the stitches with yarn or a stitch marker. Make sure the legs line up with the eyes. If the last stitch of the body is within the 14 stitches for the legs, then continue crocheting. If it is within the 3 stitches, then fasten off, leave a tail for sewing later, and rejoin the pants-colored yarn with a sl st at the back of the doll.

Rnds 1–3. Sc into each (14).

Rnd 4. {sc into 5, dec} 2 times (12).

Rnds 5–8. Sc into each (12).

Stuff the body firmly and stuff the leg as you crochet it.

Rnd 9. {sc into 4, dec} 2 times (10).

Change to the skin color.

Rnd 10. Sc into each BLO (10).

Rnds 11–12. Sc into each (10).

Stuff the leg firmly.

Rnd 13. Dec 5 times (5).

Fasten off, sew up the small hole, and weave in the ends. With the color of the pants, crochet sl sts into each front loop of round 9. For the second leg, rejoin with a sl st at the back of the doll and work the leg. When finished, sew up the hole between the legs.

Weave in the ends.

FINISHING THE SHIRT

Using the color of the shirt, join with a sl st to a front loop of round 9 at the center back of the body. Work continuously, but join with a sl st at the end of each round. Ch 1 at the beginning does not count as sc.

Rnds 1–5. Ch 1, sc into each (36).

Rnd 6. Ch 1, sl st into each (36).

Fasten off and weave in the ends.

SHIRT EMBROIDERY

The first row of the embroidery is on round 3 of the body. Using the pink yarn, pull the needle through between rounds 3 and 4, and embroider a "V" shape. Skip four stitches and pull the needle through again. Repeat, embroidering "V" shapes until you are four stitches away from the first one. Continue embroidering in the same way between rounds 4 and 6, 6 and 8, 8 and 10, and 11 and 13. Use the yellow yarn to embroider a line into the middle of each "V" shape. Weave in the ends.

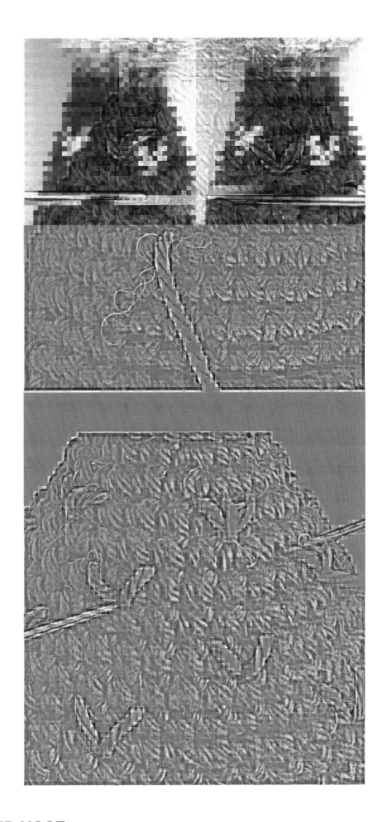

EYEBROWS AND NOSE

Using black thread, embroider the eyebrows between rounds 12 and 14. With skin-colored yarn, embroider the nose between rounds 18 and 19.

SHOES

Use the color of the shoes, make two.

Rnd 1. Ch 4, 2 sc into 2nd ch from hook, sc, 3 sc into next. Continue working on the other side of the foundation chain: sc, 2 sc into last (9).

Rnd 2. Inc 2 times, sc, inc 3 times, sc, inc 2 times (16).

Rnd 3. Sc into each BLO (16).

Rnd 4. Sc into 5, dec 3 times, sc into 5 (13).

Rnd 5. Sc into 5, dec, sc into 6 (12).

Fasten off and leave a long tail for sewing. Add stuffing to the toe of the shoes, position them on the legs, and sew them into place. Weave in the ends.

ARMS

Start with the skin color, make two.

Rnd 1. 6 sc into magic ring (6).

Rnd 2. {sc, inc} 3 times (9).

Rnd 3. Sc into each (9).

Rnd 4. {sc, dec} 3 times (6).

Rnds 5–7. Sc into each (6).

Change to the color of the shirt.

Rnds 8–12. Sc into each (6).

Fasten off and leave a long tail for sewing. Position an arm on each side of the doll and sew them into place.

HAIR

Use the hair color.

Rnd 1. 6 sc into magic ring (6).

Rnd 2. 2 sc into each (12).

Rnd 3. {sc, inc} 6 times (18).

Rnd 4. {sc into 2, inc} 6 times (24).

Rnd 5. {sc into 3, inc} 6 times (30).

Rnd 6. {sc into 4, inc} 6 times (36).

Rnd 7. {sc into 5, inc} 6 times (42).

Rnd 8. {sc into 6, inc} 6 times (48).

Rnd 9. {sc into 7, inc} 6 times (54).

Rnds 10–17. Sc into each (54).

Rnd 18. Sc into next, sl st into next 2, hdc into next 2, dc into next 47, hdc into next 2 (54).

Fasten off and leave a long tail for sewing.

PONYTAIL

Using the hair color, ch 22, sl st into 2nd ch from hook and into each ch. Join this strand to the back of the hair with a sl st between rounds 15 and 16. * Ch 22, sl st into 2nd ch from hook and into each ch. Join to the hair with a sl st next to the previous strand. Repeat from * 4 times. Fasten off and leave a long tail. Wrap yarn around the ponytail a few times close to the hair. Weave in the ends. Place the hair on the head, secure it with pins, and sew it into place.

HEADSCARF

Start with the pink headscarf yarn. Work in rows, turning at the end of each row. Ch 2 at the beginning does not count as hdc.

Row 1. Ch 7, hdc into 2nd ch from hook and into next 4 (5).

Rows 2–12. Ch 2, hdc into each (5).

Row 13. Ch 2, {hdc, inc} 2 times, hdc into last (7).

Rows 14–17. Ch 2, hdc into each (7).

Row 18. Ch 2, {hdc, inc} 3 times, hdc into last (10).

Rows 19–21. Ch 2, hdc into each (10).

Row 22. Ch 2, {hdc, inc} 5 times (15).

Row 23. Ch 2, hdc into each (15).

Row 24. Ch 2, {hdc, inc} 3 times, hdc into 9 (18).

Row 25. Ch 2, hdc into each (18).

Row 26. Ch 2, {hdc into 2, inc} 3 times, hdc into 9 (21).

Rows 27–29. Ch 2, hdc into each (21).

Row 30. Ch 2, {hdc, inc} 3 times, hdc into 15 (24).

Rows 31–35. Ch 2, hdc into each (24).

Row 36. Ch 2, {hdc, dec} 3 times, hdc into 15 (21).

Rows 37–39. Ch 2, hdc into each (21).

Row 40. Ch 2, {hdc into 2, dec} 3 times, hdc into 9 (18).

Row 41. Ch 2, hdc into each (18).

Row 42. Ch 2, {hdc, dec} 3 times, hdc into 9 (15).

Row 43. Ch 2, hdc into each (15).

Row 44. Ch 2, {hdc, dec} 5 times (10).

Rows 45–47. Ch 2, hdc into each (10).

Row 48. Ch 2, {hdc, dec} 3 times, hdc into last (7).

Rows 49–53. Ch 2, hdc into each (7).

Row 54. Ch 2, {hdc, dec} 2 times, hdc into last (5).

Rows 55–66. Ch 2, hdc into each (5).

Change to the yellow headscarf yarn. Without turning the piece, start crocheting evenly along the straight edge of the scarf (working toward the left). Crochet 24 sc evenly on 24 rows of the scarf (if you place the scarf in front of you, there are two rows between two horizontal lines). Dec 10 times on 20 rows of the scarf, then crochet 24 sc evenly on 24 rows of the scarf. This will be the bottom edge of the scarf. Continue crocheting sc evenly on the side, front, and the other side. Join with a sl st into the first sc. Fasten off and weave in the ends.

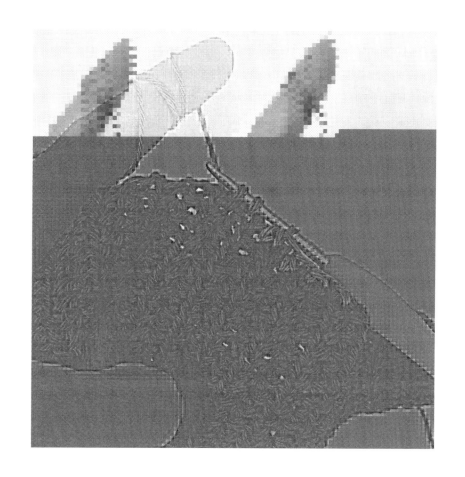

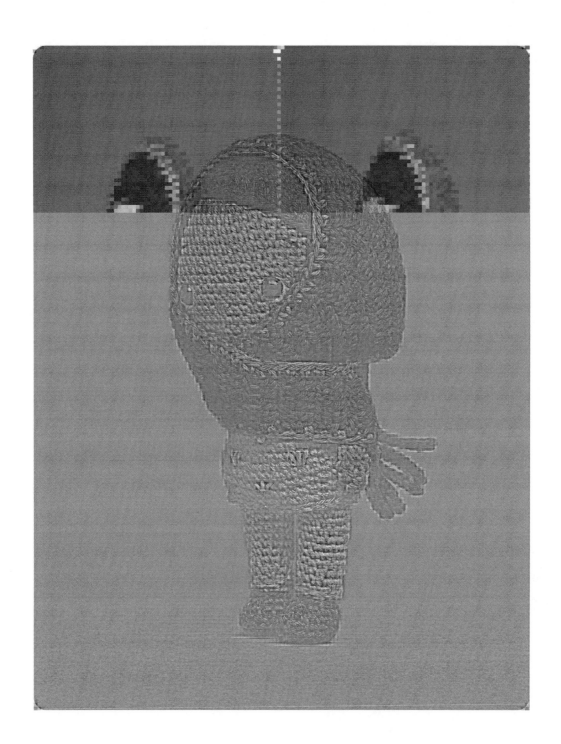

AUDREY HEPBURN

It's almost impossible not to admire the British actress and humanitarian Audrey Hepburn. She was one of the most successful actresses of the Golden Age of Hollywood, winning an Oscar for her very first starring role in *Roman Holiday*, and following it up with amazing performances in films such as *Sabrina, Breakfast at Tiffany's*, and *My Fair Lady*. She was and still is a style icon—she was the muse of Givenchy—and her signature looks, the black turtleneck, black trousers, ballet flats, and the little black dress, are still so stylish today. In later life she became a goodwill ambassador for UNICEF and devoted her time to humanitarian projects.

MATERIALS

B-1 or C-2 (2.5 mm) crochet hook

$5/16$" (8 mm) safety eyes

Tapestry needle

Polyester fiberfill

Black thread for embroidery

$5/8$ x 16" (1.5 x 40 cm) satin ribbon

Small amount of white felt

YARNS

Scheepjes Catona 100% cotton yarn:

130 Old Lace—skin, 25 g

110 Jet Black—dress, hat, shoes, 25 g

162 Black Coffee—hair, 20 g

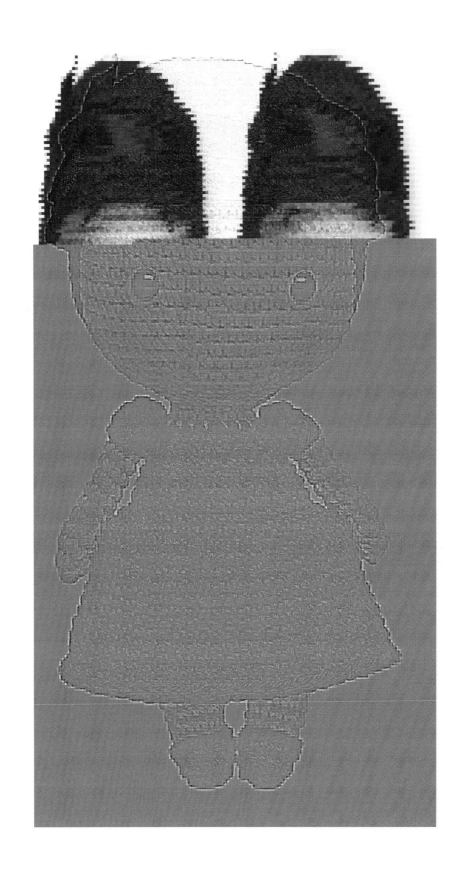

HEAD

Start with the skin color.

Rnd 1. 6 sc into magic ring (6).

Rnd 2. 2 sc into each (12).

Rnd 3. {sc, inc} 6 times (18).

Rnd 4. {sc into 2, inc} 6 times (24).

Rnd 5. {sc into 3, inc} 6 times (30).

Rnd 6. {sc into 4, inc} 6 times (36).

Rnd 7. {sc into 5, inc} 6 times (42).

Rnd 8. {sc into 6, inc} 6 times (48).

Rnd 9. {sc into 7, inc} 6 times (54).

Rnds 10–16. Sc into each (54).

Rnd 17. {sc into 8, inc} 6 times (60).

Rnds 18–20. Sc into each (60).

Rnd 21. {sc into 8, dec} 6 times (54).

Rnd 22. {sc into 7, dec} 6 times (48).

Rnd 23. {sc into 6, dec} 6 times (42).

Rnd 24. {sc into 5, dec} 6 times (36).

Add the eyes (see here for guidance).

Rnd 25. {sc into 4, dec} 6 times (30).

Rnd 26. {sc into 3, dec} 6 times (24).

Start to stuff the head.

Rnd 27. {sc into 2, dec} 6 times (18).

Rnd 28. {sc, dec} 6 times (12).

Continue to stuff the head firmly.

Rnd 29. Sc into each FLO (12).

Do not fasten off, continue with the body.

BODY

Rnd 1. {sc, inc} 6 times (18).

Change to the color of the dress. Work each sc in an "X" shape (see here) until the the change to skin color.

Rnd 2. {sc into 2, inc} 6 times (24).

Rnd 3. Sc into each (24).

Rnd 4. {sc into 3, inc} 6 times (30).

Rnd 5. Sc into each (30).

Rnd 6. {sc into 4, inc} 6 times (36).

Rnds 7–8. Sc into each (36).

Rnd 9. Sc into each (36).

Change to the skin color.

Rnd 10. Sc into each BLO (36).

Rnds 11–12. Sc into each (36).

Rnd 13. {sc into 16, dec} 2 times (34).

Rnds 14–15. Sc into each (34).

Do not fasten off, continue with the legs. Stuff the neck and body continuously.

LEGS

To make the legs, divide the work: 14 stitches for each of the legs, and 3 stitches between the legs, both front and back. Mark the stitches with yarn or a stitch marker. Make sure the legs line up with the eyes. If the last stitch of the body is within the 14 stitches for the legs, then continue crocheting. If it is within the 3 stitches, then fasten off, leave a tail for sewing later, and rejoin the skin-colored yarn with a sl st at the back of the doll.

Rnds 1–3. Sc into each (14).

Rnd 4. {sc into 5, dec} 2 times (12).

Rnds 5–8. Sc into each (12).

Stuff the body firmly and stuff the leg as you crochet it.

Rnd 9. {sc into 4, dec} 2 times (10).

Rnds 10–12. Sc into each (10).

Stuff the leg firmly.

Rnd 13. Dec 5 times (5).

Fasten off, sew up the small hole, and weave in the ends. For the second leg, rejoin with a sl st at the back of the doll and work the leg. When finished, sew up the hole between the legs. Weave in the ends.

SKIRT

Using the color of the dress, join with a sl st to a front loop of round 9 at the center back of the body. Work continuously but join with a sl st at the end of each round. Ch 1 at the beginning does not count as sc. Work each sc in an "X" shape (see here) until the skirt is complete.

Rnd 1. Ch 1, 2 sc into each (72).

Rnds 2–3. Ch 1, sc into each (72).

Rnd 4. Ch 1, {sc into 4, dec} 12 times (60).

Rnds 5–13. Ch 1, sc into each (60).

Rnd 14. Sl st into each (60).

Fasten off and weave in the ends.

EYEBROWS AND NOSE

Using black thread, embroider the eyebrows between rounds 12 and 14. With skin-colored yarn, embroider the nose between rounds 18 and 19. You can add a cheek blush with makeup or watercolor pencil.

ARMS

Use the skin color, make two.

Rnd 1. 6 sc into magic ring (6).

Rnd 2. {sc, inc} 3 times (9).

Rnd 3. Sc into each (9).

Rnd 4. {sc into 3, dec} 3 times (6).

Rnds 5–11. Sc into each (6).

Fasten off and sew the hole closed. Weave in the ends.

DRESS SLEEVES

Use the color of the dress, make two.

Rnd 1. 6 sc into magic ring (6).

Rnd 2. {sc, inc} 3 times (9).

Rnd 3. Sc into each (9).

Fasten off and leave a long tail for sewing. Place the arms into the sleeves. Using small stitches, sew the sleeves onto the arms. Sew the sleeved arms onto the body.

SHOES

Use the color of the shoes, make two.

Rnd 1. 6 sc into magic ring (6).

Rnd 2. {sc, inc} 3 times (9).

Rnd 3. {sc into 2, inc} 3 times (12).

Rnd 4. Sc into each (12).

Fasten off and leave a long tail for sewing. Position them on the legs and sew them into place. Weave in the ends.

HAIR

Use the hair color.

Rnd 1. 6 sc into magic ring (6).

Rnd 2. 2 sc into each (12).

Rnd 3. {sc, inc} 6 times (18).

Rnd 4. {sc into 2, inc} 6 times (24).

Rnd 5. {sc into 3, inc} 6 times (30).

Rnd 6. {sc into 4, inc} 6 times (36).

Rnd 7. {sc into 5, inc} 6 times (42).

Rnd 8. {sc into 6, inc} 6 times (48).

Rnd 9. {sc into 7, inc} 6 times (54).

Rnds 10–17. Sc into each (54).

Rnd 18. Sl st into next, * ch 6, sl st into 2nd ch from hook and next 4, sl st into next on the wig. Repeat from * 3 times. ** Ch 5, sl st into 2nd ch from hook and next 3, sl st into next on the wig. Repeat from ** 2 times. *** Ch 3, sl st into 2nd ch from hook and next, sl st into next on the wig. Repeat from *** once more. Sc into next 42, sl st into last.

Fasten off and leave a long tail for sewing. Place the hair on the head, secure it with pins, and sew it into place.

BUN

Use the hair color.

Rnd 1. 6 sc into magic ring (6).

Rnd 2. 2 sc into each (12

Rnd 3. {sc, inc} 6 times (18).

Rnd 4. {sc into 2, inc} 6 times (24).

Rnd 5. {sc into 3, inc} 6 times (30).

Rnd 6. {sc into 4, inc} 6 times (36).

Rnds 7–8. Sc into each (36).

Rnd 9. {sc into 4, dec} 6 times (30).

Fasten off and leave a long tail for sewing. Place the bun on the head between rounds 9 and 18 of the hair. Secure the bun with pins, stuff it, and sew it into place.

HAT

Use the color of the hat.

Rnd 1. 7 sc into magic ring (7).

Rnd 2. 2 sc into each (14).

Rnd 3. {sc, inc} 7 times (21).

Rnd 4. {sc into 2, inc} 7 times (28).

Rnd 5. {sc into 3, inc} 7 times (35).

Rnd 6. {sc into 4, inc} 7 times (42).

Rnd 7. {sc into 5, inc} 7 times (49).

Rnd 8. {sc into 6, inc} 7 times (56).

Rnds 9–11. Sc into each (56).

Rnd 12. Hdc into each FLO of round 11 (56).

Rnd 13. Sc into each BLO of round 11 (56).

Rnd 14. {sc into 7, inc} 7 times (63).

Rnd 15. Sc into each (63).

Rnd 16. {sc into 8, inc} 7 times (70).

Rnds 17–18. Sc into each (70).

Rnd 19. Sl st into each (70).

Fasten off and weave in the ends. Using black thread, sew the center of the satin ribbon onto the back of the hat where you fastened off. Twist the ribbon and sew it onto the hat 1¾" (4.5 cm) from where you first stitched it. Twist the ribbon again and sew it onto the hat 1¾" (4.5 cm) from the previous sewn point. Repeat this twist and sew method on the other side of the hat. Tie a knot with the rest of the ribbon and trim the ends.

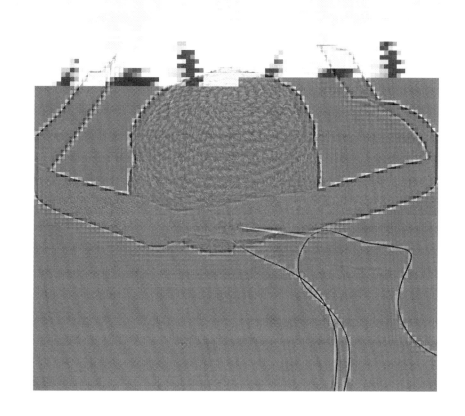

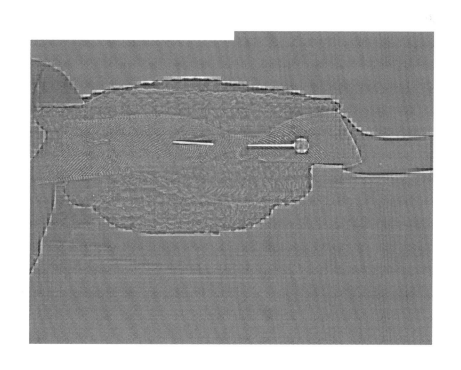

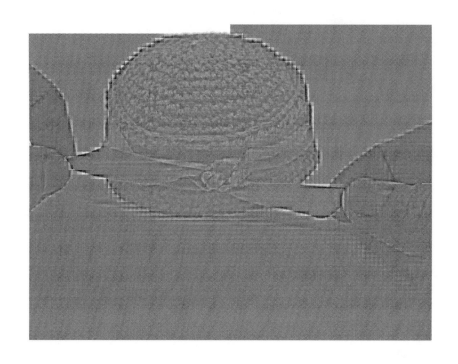

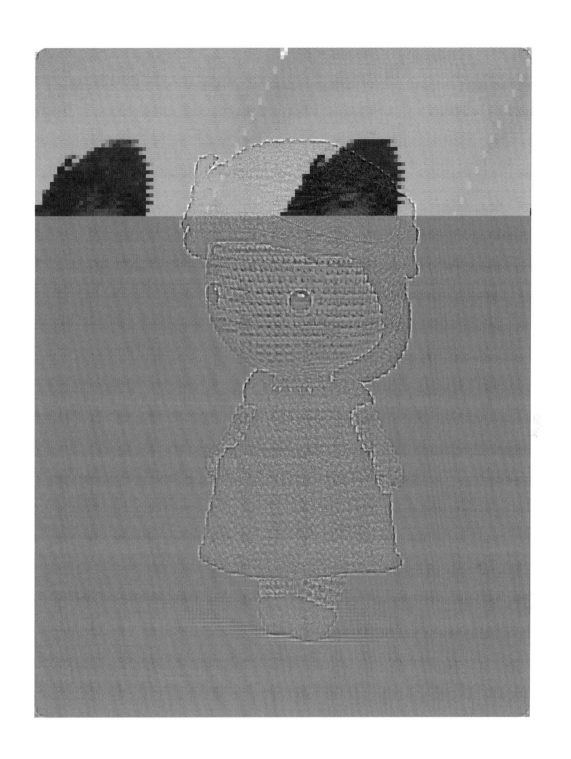

SERENA WILLIAMS

Serena Williams is undoubtedly the greatest female tennis player of all time. The American athlete has won twenty-three Grand Slam singles titles—the most of any player in the Open Era of tennis—but she is so much more than just an athlete. Serena Williams is an example of how to make a difference. She is a fighter on and off the court, who tries to change the system and fights for women's rights in sports. She gave birth to her first child in 2017 and was eight weeks pregnant when she won the Australian Open. She is a champion on and off the court—a real icon.

MATERIALS

B-1 or C-2 (2.5 mm) crochet hook

$5/_{16}$" (8 mm) safety eyes

Tapestry needle

Polyester fiberfill

Black thread for embroidery

Small amount of white felt

YARNS

Scheepjes Catona 100% cotton yarn:

507 Chocolate—skin, 20 g

258 Rosewood—dress, headband, 15 g

252 Watermelon—shoes (A), 2 g

110 Jet Black—belt, shoes (B), 3 g

106 Snow White—shoes (C), 1 g

162 Black Coffee—hair, 18 g

502 Camel—curls, 8 g

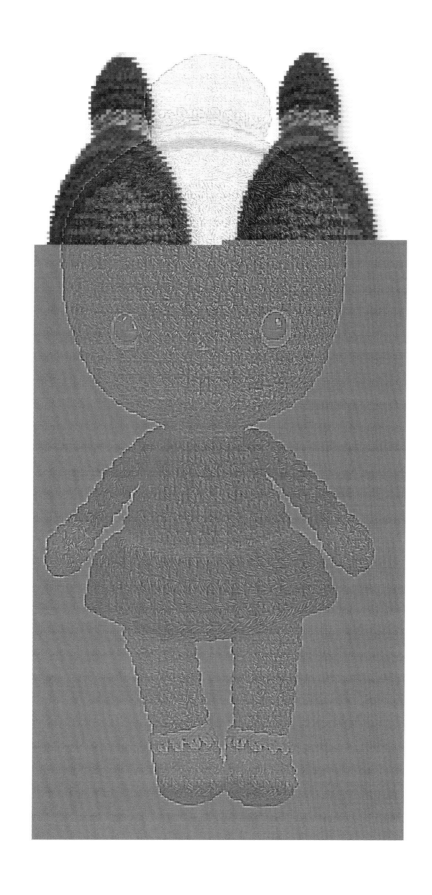

HEAD

Start with the skin color.

Rnd 1. 6 sc into magic ring (6).

Rnd 2. 2 sc into each (12).

Rnd 3. {sc, inc} 6 times (18).

Rnd 4. {sc into 2, inc} 6 times (24).

Rnd 5. {sc into 3, inc} 6 times (30).

Rnd 6. {sc into 4, inc} 6 times (36).

Rnd 7. {sc into 5, inc} 6 times (42).

Rnd 8. {sc into 6, inc} 6 times (48).

Rnd 9. {sc into 7, inc} 6 times (54).

Rnds 10–16. Sc into each (54).

Rnd 17. {sc into 8, inc} 6 times (60).

Rnds 18–20. Sc into each (60).

Rnd 21. {sc into 8, dec} 6 times (54).

Rnd 22. {sc into 7, dec} 6 times (48).

Rnd 23. {sc into 6, dec} 6 times (42).

Rnd 24. {sc into 5, dec} 6 times (36).

Add the eyes (see here for guidance).

Rnd 25. {sc into 4, dec} 6 times (30).

Rnd 26. {sc into 3, dec} 6 times (24).

Start to stuff the head.

Rnd 27. {sc into 2, dec} 6 times (18).

Rnd 28. {sc, dec} 6 times (12).

Continue to stuff the head firmly.

Rnd 29. Sc into each FLO (12).

Change to the color of the dress.

BODY

Rnd 1. {sc, inc} 6 times (18).

Rnd 2. {sc into 2, inc} 6 times (24).

Rnd 3. Sc into each (24).

Rnd 4. {sc into 3, inc} 6 times (30).

Rnd 5. Sc into each (30).

Rnd 6. {sc into 4, inc} 6 times (36).

Rnd 7. Sc into each (36).

Rnd 8. Sc into each (36).

Change to the color of the belt.

Rnd 9. Sc into each (36).

Change to the color of the dress.

Rnd 10. Sc into each BLO (36).

Rnds 11–12. Sc into each (36).

Rnd 13. {sc into 16, dec} 2 times (34).

Rnds 14–15. Sc into each (34).

Fasten off and weave in the ends. Stuff the neck and body continuously.

LEGS

To make the legs, divide the work: 14 stitches for each of the legs, and 3 stitches between the legs, both front and back. Mark the stitches with yarn or a stitch marker. Make sure the legs line up with the eyes. Use skin-colored yarn and join with a sl st at the back of the doll to start.

Rnds 1–3. Sc into each (14).

Rnd 4. {sc into 5, dec} 2 times (12).

Rnds 5–8. Sc into each (12).

Stuff the body firmly and stuff the leg as you crochet it.

Rnd 9. {sc into 4, dec} 2 times (10).

Rnds 10–12. Sc into each (10).

Stuff the leg firmly.

Rnd 13. Dec 5 times (5).

Fasten off, sew up the small hole, and weave in the ends. For the second leg, rejoin with a sl st at the back of the doll and work the leg. When finished, sew up the hole between the legs. Weave in the ends.

SKIRT

Using the color of the dress, join with a sl st to a front loop of round 9 at the center back of the body. Work continuously but join with a sl st at the end of each round. Ch 2 at the beginning does not count as dc.

Rnd 1. Ch 2, {dc, inc} 18 times (54).

Rnd 2. Ch 2, dc into each (54).

Rnd 3. Ch 2, hdc into each (54).

Rnd 4. Sl st into each (54).

Fasten off and weave in the ends.

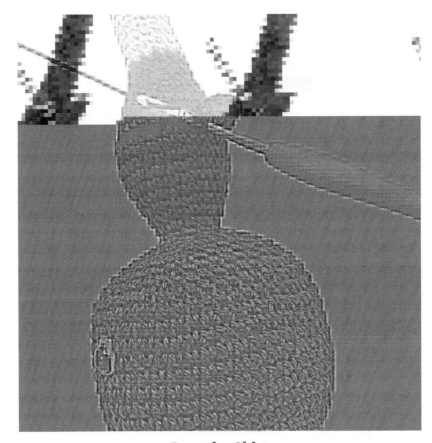

Round 1, Skirt

EYEBROWS AND NOSE

Using black thread, embroider the eyebrows between rounds 12 and 14. With skin-colored yarn, embroider the nose between rounds 18 and 19.

ARMS

Start with the skin color, make two.

Rnd 1. 6 sc into magic ring (6).

Rnd 2. {sc, inc} 3 times (9).

Rnd 3. Sc into each (9).

Rnd 4. {sc into 1, dec} 3 times (6).

Change to the color of the dress.

Rnds 5–12. Sc into each (6).

Fasten off and leave a long tail for sewing. Position an arm on each side of the doll and sew them into place.

SHOES

Start with shoe color A, make two.

Rnd 1. Ch 4, 2 sc into 2nd ch from hook, sc, 3 sc into next. Continue working on the other side of the foundation chain: sc, 2 sc into last (9).

Rnd 2. Inc 2 times, sc, inc 3 times, sc, inc 2 times (16). Change to shoe color B.

Rnd 3. Sc into each BLO (16).

Rnd 4. Sc into 5, dec 3 times, sc into 5 (13).

Rnd 5. Sc into 6, dec, sc into 5 (12).

Change to shoe color C.

Rnd 6. Sc into each (12).

Fasten off and leave a long tail for sewing. Add stuffing to the toe of the shoes, position them on the legs, and sew them into place. Weave in the ends.

HAIR

Use the dark brown hair color.

Rnd 1. 6 sc into magic ring (6).

Rnd 2. 2 sc into each (12).

Rnd 3. {sc, inc} 6 times (18).

Rnd 4. {sc into 2, inc} 6 times (24).

Rnd 5. {sc into 3, inc} 6 times (30).

Rnd 6. {sc into 4, inc} 6 times (36).

Rnd 7. {sc into 5, inc} 6 times (42).

Rnd 8. {sc into 6, inc} 6 times (48).

Rnd 9. {sc into 7, inc} 6 times (54).

Rnds 10–19. Sc into each (54).

Fasten off and leave a long tail for sewing. Place the hair on the head, secure it with pins, and sew it into place.

BUN

Use the dark brown hair color.

Rnd 1. 6 sc into magic ring (6).

Rnd 2. 2 sc into each (12).

Rnd 3. {sc, inc} 6 times (18).

Rnd 4. {sc into 2, inc} 6 times (24).

Rnd 5. {sc into 3, inc} 6 times (30).

Rnds 6–7. Sc into each (30).

Change to the lighter curls color.

Rnds 8–9. Sc into each (30).

Fasten off and leave a long tail for sewing.

CURLS

Use the color of the curls, make five.

Ch 32, 2 hdc into 3rd ch from hook and next 27, sc into last 2. Fasten off and leave a long tail for sewing. Place three of the curls on top of the head at about round 2 of the hair. Place them as close together as possible so that the bun will cover the tops of the curls. Sew the three curls into place. Place the other two curls on top of the first three and sew them on. Weave in the ends. Slightly stuff the bun and position it on the head so that half of the bun covers the tops of the curls and half lies on the hair. Continue to stuff the bun while you sew it into place.

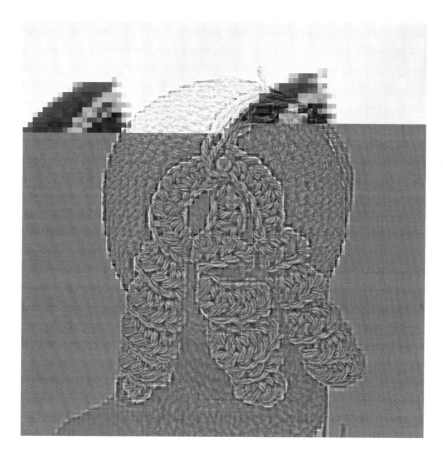

HAIRBAND

Use the dress color. Leave a long tail at the beginning, then ch 28. Fasten off and leave a long tail. Wrap the chain around the bun and tie a knot below the curls. Weave in the ends.

HEADBAND

Use the dress color. Leave a long tail at the beginning, then ch 70. Fasten off and leave a long tail. Wrap the chain around the head between rounds 13 and 14 and sew both ends to the hair, next to each other. Weave in the ends.

MUHAMMAD ALI

American Muhammad Ali was one of the most influential athletes in the history of sport. For many, he was and still is the greatest boxer of all time, but he was also an activist who fought for equal rights. Ali was the first fighter to win the world heavyweight championship on three separate occasions, and he defended his title nineteen times. In 1961 he converted to Islam and became a Muslim, which defined not only his life but also his sporting career. He refused to be drafted into the military and fight in Vietnam, and as a result was stripped of his titles and suspended from boxing for four years—but he fought his way back to the top and became champion again.

MATERIALS

B-1 or C-2 (2.5 mm) crochet hook

$^5/_{16}$" (8 mm) safety eyes

Tapestry needle

Polyester fiberfill

Black thread for embroidery

Small amount of white felt

YARNS

Scheepjes Catona 100% cotton yarn:

507 Chocolate—skin, 25 g

106 Snow White—shorts, shoes, 10 g

110 Jet Black—hair, belt, 18 g

115 Hot Red—boxing gloves, 8 g

HEAD

Start with the skin color.

Rnd 1. 6 sc into magic ring (6).

Rnd 2. 2 sc into each (12).

Rnd 3. {sc, inc} 6 times (18).

Rnd 4. {sc into 2, inc} 6 times (24).

Rnd 5. {sc into 3, inc} 6 times (30).

Rnd 6. {sc into 4, inc} 6 times (36).

Rnd 7. {sc into 5, inc} 6 times (42).

Rnd 8. {sc into 6, inc} 6 times (48).

Rnd 9. {sc into 7, inc} 6 times (54).

Rnds 10–16. Sc into each (54).

Rnd 17. {sc into 8, inc} 6 times (60).

Rnds 18–20. Sc into each (60).

Rnd 21. {sc into 8, dec} 6 times (54).

Rnd 22. {sc into 7, dec} 6 times (48).

Rnd 23. {sc into 6, dec} 6 times (42).

Rnd 24. {sc into 5, dec} 6 times (36).

Add the eyes (see here for guidance).

Rnd 25. {sc into 4, dec} 6 times (30).

Rnd 26. {sc into 3, dec} 6 times (24).

Start to stuff the head.

Rnd 27. {sc into 2, dec} 6 times (18).

Rnd 28. {sc, dec} 6 times (12).

Continue to stuff the head firmly.

Rnd 29. Sc into each FLO (12).

Do not fasten off, continue with the body.

BODY

Rnd 1. {sc, inc} 6 times (18).

Rnd 2. {sc into 2, inc} 6 times (24).

Rnd 3. Sc into each (24).

Rnd 4. {sc into 3, inc} 6 times (30).

Rnd 5. Sc into each (30).

Rnd 6. {sc into 4, inc} 6 times (36).

Rnd 7. Sc into each (36).

Rnd 8. Sc into each (36).

Change to the color of the belt.

Rnd 9. Hdc into each (36).

Change to the skin color.

Rnd 10. Sc into each BLO (36).

Rnds 11–12. Sc into each (36).

Rnd 13. {sc into 16, dec} 2 times (34).

Rnd 14. Sc into each (34).

Do not fasten off, continue with the legs. Stuff the neck and body continuously.

LEGS

To make the legs, divide the work: 14 stitches for each of the legs, and 3 stitches between the legs, both front and back. Mark the stitches with yarn or a stitch marker. Make sure the legs line up with the eyes. If the last stitch of the body is within the 14 stitches for the legs, then continue crocheting. If it is within the 3 stitches, then fasten off, leave a tail for sewing later, and rejoin the skin-colored yarn with a sl st at the back of the doll.

Rnds 1–3. Sc into each (14).

Rnd 4. {sc into 5, dec} 2 times (12).

Rnds 5–8. Sc into each (12).

Stuff the body firmly and stuff the leg as you crochet it.

Rnd 9. {sc into 4, dec} 2 times (10).

Rnds 10–12. Sc into each (10).

Stuff the leg firmly.

Rnd 13. Dec 5 times (5).

Fasten off, sew up the small hole, and weave in the ends. For the second leg, rejoin with a sl st at the back of the doll and work the leg. When finished, sew up the hole between the legs. Weave in the ends.

EYEBROWS AND NOSE

Using black thread, embroider the eyebrows between rounds 12 and 14. With skin-colored yarn, embroider the nose between rounds 18 and 19.

SHORTS

Using the color of the shorts, join with a sl st to a front loop of round 9 at the center back of the body. Work continuously but join with a sl st at the end of each round. Ch 1 at the beginning does not count as sc.

Rnd 1. Ch 1, {sc, inc} 18 times. (54).

Rnds 2–4. Ch 1, sc into each. (54).

Rnd 5. Ch 1, {sc into 4, dec} 9 times. (45).

Rnd 6. Ch 1, sc into each. (45).

Rnd 7. Ch 1, dec, sc into each. (44).

Do not fasten off. Divide the piece into two sections of 22 stitches to form the legs of the shorts. Make sure to align the middle of the shorts with the doll's legs, nose, and eyes. Now work each shorts leg continuously, but without joining each round with a sl st.

162

SHORTS LEGS

Rnd 1. Sc into each (22).

Fasten off and weave in the ends. Rejoin to the shorts at the back of the doll for the other shorts leg and repeat round 1.Fasten off and weave in the ends.

ARMS AND BOXING GLOVES

LEFT

Start with the color of the boxing gloves.

Rnd 1. Ch 3, 2 sc into 2nd ch from hook, 3 sc into next.

Continue on the other side of the foundation chain: sc into last (6).

Rnd 2. {inc, sc into next} 3 times (9).

Rnd 3. {sc into 2, inc} 3 times (12).

Rnds 4–5. Sc into each (12).

Rnd 6. Sc into next, 4 hdc into next and form a popcorn stitch (see here), sc into 10 (12).

Rnd 7. {sc into 2, dec} 3 times (9).

Rnd 8. {sc into 2, dec} 2 times, sc into last (7).

Change to the skin color.

Rnds 9–15. Sc into each (7).

Fasten off and leave a long tail for sewing. Using a needle and the red yarn, pull together the palm part of the glove.

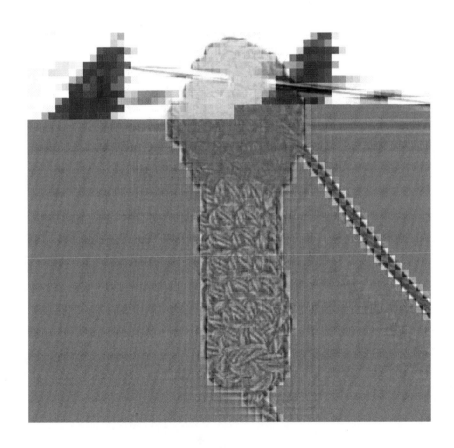

RIGHT Start with the color of the boxing gloves.

Rnd 1. Ch 3, 2 sc into 2nd ch from hook, 3 sc into next. Continue on the other side of the foundation chain: sc into last (6).

Rnd 2. {inc, sc into next} 3 times (9).

Rnd 3. {sc into 2, inc} 3 times (12).

Rnds 4–5. Sc into each (12).

Rnd 6. Sc into 6, 4 hdc into next and form a popcorn stitch (see here), sc into 5 (12).

Rnd 7. {dec, sc into 2} 3 times (9).

Rnd 8. {sc into 2, dec} 2 times, sc into last (7).

Change to the skin color.

Rnds 9–15. Sc into each (7).

Fasten off and leave a long tail for sewing. Using a needle and the red yarn, pull together the palm part of the glove. Position an arm on each side of the doll and sew them into place.

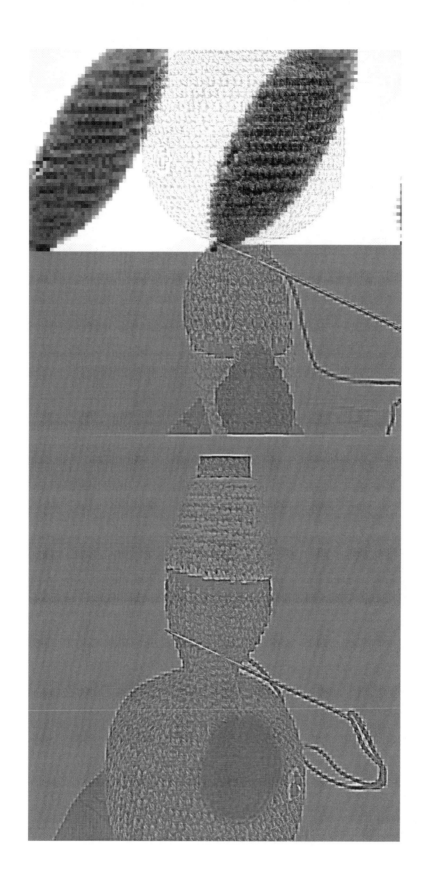

SHOES

Use the color of the shoes, make two.

Rnd 1. Ch 4, 2 sc into 2nd ch from hook, sc, 3 sc into next. Continue working on the other side of the foundation chain: sc, 2 sc into last (9).

Rnd 2. Inc 2 times, sc, inc 3 times, sc, inc 2 times (16).

Rnd 3. Sc into each BLO (16).

Rnd 4. Sc into 5, dec 3 times, sc into 5 (13).

Rnd 5. Sc into 6, dec, sc into 5 (12).

Rnds 6–7. Sc into each (12).

Fasten off and leave a long tail for sewing. Add stuffing to the toe of the shoes, position them on the legs, and sew them into place. Weave in the ends.

HAIR

Use the hair color.

Rnd 1. 6 sc into magic ring (6).

Rnd 2. 2 sc in each (12).

Rnd 3. {sc, inc} 6 times (18).

Rnd 4. {sc into 2, inc} 6 times (24).

Rnd 5. {sc into 3, inc} 6 times (30).

Rnd 6. {sc into 4, inc} 6 times (36).

Rnd 7. {sc into 5, inc} 6 times (42).

Rnd 8. {sc into 6, inc} 6 times (48).

Rnd 9. {sc into 7, inc} 6 times (54).

Rnds 10–17. Sc into each (54).

Rnd 18. Sc into 16, hdc into next 4, sl st into next 2, hdc into next 2, dc into next 6, hdc into next 2, sl st into next 2, hdc into next 4, sc into next 16.

Rnd 19. Sc into 6, sl st into next.

Fasten off and leave a long tail for sewing. Place the hair on the head, secure it with pins, and sew it into place.

GANDHI

Mohandas Karamchand Gandhi was one of the greatest spiritual and political leaders of the twentieth century. He is also honored by Indians as the father of the Indian nation. Gandhi was a lawyer, a politician, and a social activist who became the leader of the nationalist movement against the British rule of India. He helped free the Indian people through nonviolent resistance, which later inspired civil rights activists, including Martin Luther King, Jr. and Nelson Mandela.

MATERIALS

B-1 or C-2 (2.5 mm) crochet hook

$5/16$" (8 mm) safety eyes

Tapestry needle

Polyester fiberfill

Black thread for embroidery

Small amount of white felt

18 gauge (1 mm) floral stem wire

Round-nose pliers

YARNS

Scheepjes Catona 100% cotton yarn:

502 Camel—skin, 35 g

106 Snow White—dhoti, shawl, 20 g

507 Chocolate—shoes, 3 g

074 Mercury—moustache, 1 g

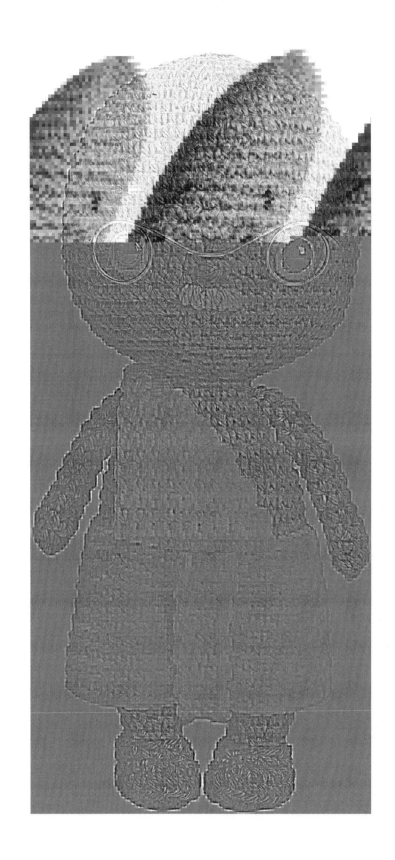

HEAD

Start with the skin color.

Rnd 1. 6 sc into magic ring (6).

Rnd 2. 2 sc into each (12).

Rnd 3. {sc, inc} 6 times (18).

Rnd 4. {sc into 2, inc} 6 times (24).

Rnd 5. {sc into 3, inc} 6 times (30).

Rnd 6. {sc into 4, inc} 6 times (36).

Rnd 7. {sc into 5, inc} 6 times (42).

Rnd 8. {sc into 6, inc} 6 times (48).

Rnd 9. {sc into 7, inc} 6 times (54).

Rnds 10–16. Sc into each (54).

Rnd 17. {sc into 8, inc} 6 times (60).

Rnds 18–20. Sc into each (60).

Rnd 21. {sc into 8, dec} 6 times (54).

Rnd 22. {sc into 7, dec} 6 times (48).

Rnd 23. {sc into 6, dec} 6 times (42).

Rnd 24. {sc into 5, dec} 6 times (36).

Add the eyes (see here for guidance).

Rnd 25. {sc into 4, dec} 6 times (30).

Rnd 26. {sc into 3, dec} 6 times (24).

Start to stuff the head.

Rnd 27. {sc into 2, dec} 6 times (18).

Rnd 28. {sc, dec} 6 times (12).

Continue to stuff the head firmly.

Rnd 29. Sc into each FLO (12).

Do not fasten off, continue with the body.

BODY

Rnd 1. {sc, inc} 6 times (18).

Rnd 2. {sc into 2, inc} 6 times (24).

Rnd 3. Sc into each (24).

Rnd 4. {sc into 3, inc} 6 times (30).

Rnd 5. Sc into each (30).

Rnd 6. {sc into 4, inc} 6 times (36).

Rnds 7–10. Sc into each (36).

Rnd 11. Sc into each BLO (36).

Rnd 12. Sc into each (36).

Rnd 13. {sc into 16, dec} 2 times (34).

Rnds 14–15. Sc into each (34).

Do not fasten off, continue with the legs. Stuff the neck and body continuously.

LEGS

To make the legs, divide the work: 14 stitches for each of the legs, and 3 stitches between the legs, both front and back. Mark the stitches with yarn or a stitch marker. Make sure the legs line up with the eyes. If the last stitch of the body is within the 14 stitches for the legs, then continue crocheting. If it is within the 3 stitches, then fasten off, leave a tail for sewing later, and rejoin the skin-colored yarn with a sl st at the back of the doll.

Rnds 1–3. Sc into each (14).

Rnd 4. {sc into 5, dec} 2 times (12).

Rnds 5–8. Sc into each (12).

Stuff the body firmly and stuff the leg as you crochet it.

Rnd 9. {sc into 4, dec} 2 times (10).

Rnds 10–12. Sc into each (10).

Stuff the leg firmly.

Rnd 13. Dec 5 times (5).

Fasten off, sew up the small hole, and weave in the ends. For the second leg, rejoin with a sl st at the back of the doll and work the leg. When finished, sew up the hole between the legs. Weave in the ends.

DHOTI

Using the color of the dhoti, join with a sl st to a front loop of round 10 at the center back of the body. Work continuously, but join with a sl st at the end of each round. Ch 1 at the beginning does not count as sc.

Rnd 1. Ch 1, sc into each (36).

Rnd 2. Ch 1, BLO {sc into 2, inc} 12 times (48).

Rnds 3–11. Ch 1, BLO sc into each (48).

Fasten off and weave in the ends.

ARMS

Use the skin color, make two.

Rnd 1. 6 sc into magic ring (6).

Rnd 2. {sc, inc} 3 times (9).

Rnd 3. Sc into each (9).

Rnd 4. {sc into 2, dec} 2 times, sc into last (7).

Rnds 5–12. Sc into each (7).

Fasten off and leave a long tail for sewing. Position an arm on each side of the doll and sew them into place.

SHAWL

Use the color of the shawl. Use pins to mark the position of the shawl by placing two pins in line with the eyes into the front loops of round 1 of the dhoti, 10 stitches apart. Start crocheting from the right side, joining with a sl st to the front loop of round 1 of the dhoti at the first pin. Work in rows, turning at the end of each row. Ch 1 at the beginning does not count as sc.

Row 1. Sc into each front loop of round 1 of dhoti between pins, turn (10).

Row 2. Ch 1, sc into each, turn (10).

Row 3. Ch 1, sk first st, sc into 9, turn (9).

Row 4. Ch 1, sc into each, turn (9).

Row 5. Ch 1, sk first st, sc into 8, turn (8).

Row 6. Ch 1, sc into each, turn (8).

Row 7. Ch 1, sk first st, sc into 7, turn (7).

Row 8. Ch 1, sc into 5, dec, turn (6).

Row 9. Ch 1, sk first st, sc into 5, turn (5).

Row 10. Ch 1, sc into 3, dec, turn (4).

Row 11. Ch 1, sk first st, sc into 3, turn (3).

Row 12. Ch 1, sc, dec, turn (2).

Rows 13–16. Ch 1, sc into each, turn (2).

Row 17. Ch 1, inc, sc into last, turn (3).

Row 18. Ch 1, sc into 2, inc, turn (4).

Row 19. Ch 1, inc, sc into 3, turn (5).

Row 20. Ch 1, sc into 4, inc, turn (6).

Row 21. Ch 1, inc, sc into 5, turn (7).

Row 22. Ch 1, sc into 6, inc, turn (8).

Row 23. Ch 1, sc into each, turn (8).

Row 24. Ch 1, sc into 7, inc, turn (9).

Row 25. Ch 1, sc into each, turn (9).

Row 26. Ch 1, sc into 8, inc (10).

Fasten off and leave a long tail for sewing. Use two pins to secure the back part of the shawl onto the dhoti and sew it to the front loops of round 1.

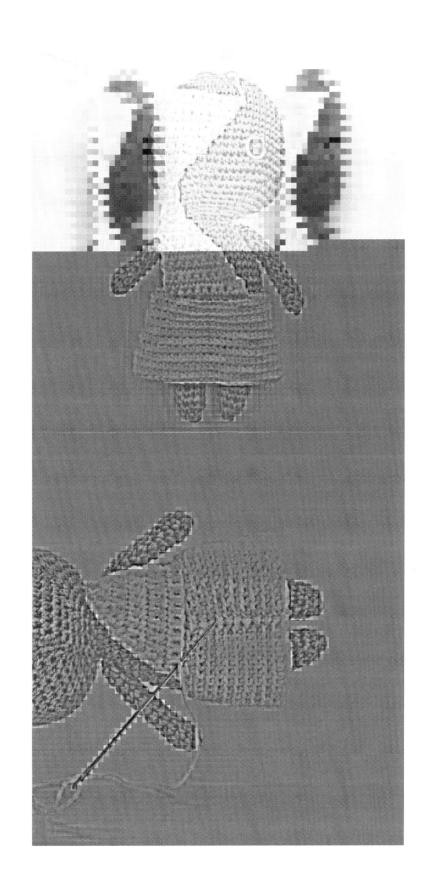

FINISHING THE DHOTI

Crochet a strip using the color of the dhoti. Start by leaving a long tail.

Row 1. Ch 4, sc into 2nd ch from hook and next 2, turn (3).

Rows 2–24. Ch 1, sc into each, turn (3).

Fasten off and leave a long tail. Place the strip between the legs and sew it to round 1 of the dhoti on both front and back, right below the shawl. Weave in the ends.

EYEBROWS, NOSE, AND MUSTACHE

With skin-colored yarn, embroider the nose between rounds 18 and 19. Mark the position of the mustache with four pins. Place two pins on either side of the nose between rounds 19 and 20. Place two more pins between rounds 20 and 21 one stitch away from the previous pins. Using gray yarn, embroider the mustache between the pins. With black thread, embroider the eyebrows between rounds 13 and 15.

SHOES

Use the color of the shoes, make two.

Rnd 1. Ch 4, 2 sc into 2nd ch from hook, sc, 3 sc into next. Continue working on the other side of the foundation chain: sc, 2 sc into last (9).

Rnd 2. Inc 2 times, sc, inc 3 times, sc, inc 2 times (16).

Rnd 3. Sc into each BLO (16).

Rnd 4. Sc into 5, dec 3 times, sc into 5 (13).

Rnd 5. Sc into 6, dec, sc into 5 (12).

Fasten off and leave a long tail for sewing. Add stuffing to the toe of the shoes, position them on the legs, and sew them into place. Weave in the ends.

GLASSES

Take the floral wire and find a round object to use to form the ring shape for the glasses. I used the plastic part of a thread spool, with a ½" (1.5 cm) diameter. Wrap the longer end of the wire around the spool, leaving 1½" (4 cm) on the shorter end. Wrap the wire all the way around the spool. For the other ring of the glasses, measure 1¾" (4.5 cm) from the first ring on the longer end of the wire and wrap it around the spool again. Use the spool to shape the curved bridge of the glasses. Bend the stems at right angles and place the glasses on the doll. Insert the stems into the head four stitches away from the eyes between rounds 16 and 17.

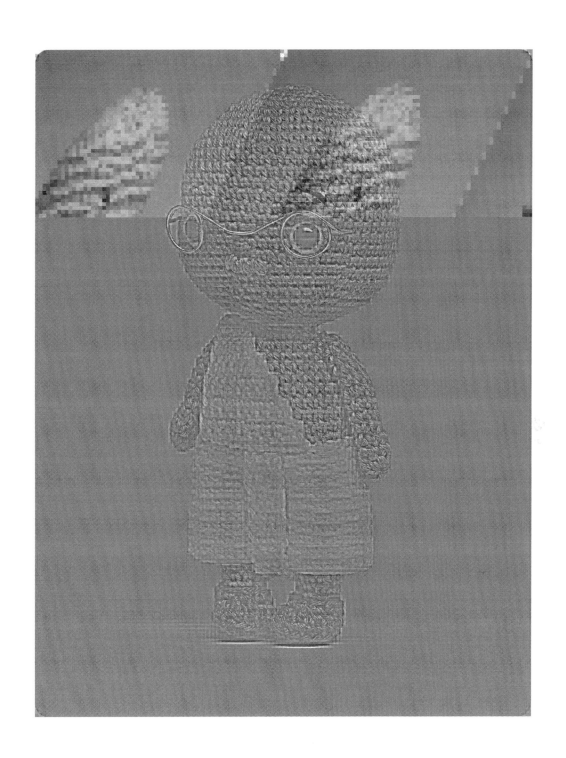

PRINCE

Genius, talent, composer, icon, inspiration, the purple master, visionary—just a few of Prince's qualities. Prince Rogers Nelson was an American singer-songwriter, a multi-instrumentalist, and one of the greatest musicians of his generation. Coming from a musical family, he played the piano by the age of seven and had a record deal by the age of nineteen. He always said that he was going to play all kinds of music, and not be judged for the color of his skin but for the quality of his work—and he remained true to himself. He was always on the cutting edge and his music integrated multiple styles, including funk, soul, pop, rock, R&B, and jazz. He was and still is an inspiration for musicians and entertainers of all ages and genres.

MATERIALS

B-1 or C-2 (2.5 mm) crochet hook

$5/16$" (8 mm) safety eyes

Tapestry needle

Polyester fiberfill

Black thread for embroidery

Small amount of white felt

YARNS

Scheepjes Catona 100% cotton yarn:

503 Hazelnut—skin, 20 g

106 Snow White—shirt, 10 g

110 Jet Black—hair, pants, 50 g

113 Delphinium—coat, shoes, 18 g

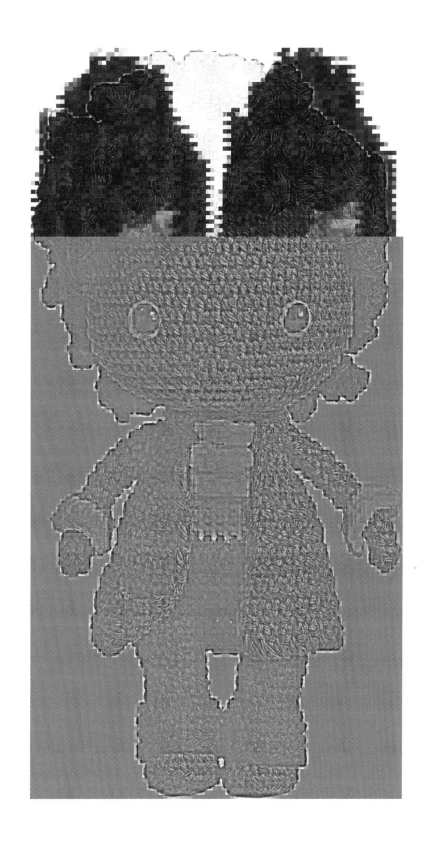

HEAD

Start with the skin color.

Rnd 1. 6 sc into magic ring (6).

Rnd 2. 2 sc into each (12).

Rnd 3. {sc, inc} 6 times (18).

Rnd 4. {sc into 2, inc} 6 times (24).

Rnd 5. {sc into 3, inc} 6 times (30).

Rnd 6. {sc into 4, inc} 6 times (36).

Rnd 7. {sc into 5, inc} 6 times (42).

Rnd 8. {sc into 6, inc} 6 times (48).

Rnd 9. {sc into 7, inc} 6 times (54).

Rnds 10–16. Sc into each (54).

Rnd 17. {sc into 8, inc} 6 times (60).

Rnds 18–20. Sc into each (60).

Rnd 21. {sc into 8, dec} 6 times (54).

Rnd 22. {sc into 7, dec} 6 times (48).

Rnd 23. {sc into 6, dec} 6 times (42).

Rnd 24. {sc into 5, dec} 6 times (36).

Add the eyes (see here for guidance).

Rnd 25. {sc into 4, dec} 6 times (30).

Rnd 26. {sc into 3, dec} 6 times (24).

Start to stuff the head.

Rnd 27. {sc into 2, dec} 6 times (18).

Rnd 28. {sc, dec} 6 times (12).

Continue to stuff the head firmly.

Rnd 29. Sc into each FLO (12).

Change to the color of the shirt.

BODY

Rnd 1. {sc, inc} 6 times (18).

Rnd 2. BLO {sc into 2, inc} 6 times (24).

Rnd 3. BLO sc into each (24).

Rnd 4. BLO {sc into 3, inc} 6 times (30).

Rnd 5. BLO sc into each (30).

Rnd 6. BLO {sc into 4, inc} 6 times (36).

Rnd 7. BLO sc into each (36).

Rnd 8. BLO sc into each (36).

Change to the color of the pants.

Rnds 9–12. Sc into each (36).

Rnd 13. {sc into 16, dec} 2 times (34).

Rnds 14–15. Sc into each (34).

Do not fasten off, continue with the legs. Stuff the neck and body continuously.

LEGS

To make the legs, divide the work: 14 stitches for each of the legs, and 3 stitches between the legs, both front and back. Mark the stitches with yarn or a stitch marker. Make sure the legs line up with the eyes. If the last stitch of the body is within the 14 stitches for the legs, then continue crocheting. If it is within the 3 stitches, then fasten off, leave a tail for sewing later, and rejoin the pants-colored yarn with a sl st at the back of the doll.

Rnds 1–3. Sc into each (14).

Rnd 4. {sc into 5, dec} 2 times (12).

Rnds 5–8. Sc into each (12).

Stuff the body firmly and stuff the leg as you crochet it.

Rnd 9. {sc into 4, dec} 2 times BLO (10).

Rnds 10–12. Sc into each (10).

Stuff the leg firmly.

Rnd 13. Dec 5 times (5).

Fasten off, sew up the small hole, and weave in the ends. For the second leg, rejoin with a sl st at the back of the doll and work the leg. When finished, sew up the hole between the legs. Weave in the ends.

PANTS

To make the bell-bottom flares, join the black yarn with a sl st to a front loop of round 8 at the back of one leg.

Rnd 1. Ch 1, {sc, inc} 6 times (18).

Rnds 2–4. Sc into each (18).

Fasten off, weave in the ends, and repeat with the other leg.

SHOES

Use the color of the shoes, make two.

Rnd 1. Ch 4, 2 sc into 2nd ch from hook, sc, 3 sc into next. Continue working on the other side of the foundation chain: sc, 2 sc into last (9).

Rnd 2. Inc 2 times, sc, inc 3 times, sc, inc 2 times (16).

Rnd 3. Sc into each BLO (16).

Rnd 4. Sc into 5, dec 3 times, sc into 5 (13).

Rnd 5. Sc into 6, dec, sc into 5 (12).

Fasten off and leave a long tail for sewing. Add stuffing to the toe of the shoes, turn up the bottom of the pants, position the shoes on the legs, and sew them into place. Weave in the ends.

SHIRT NECK FRILLS

Use the color of the shirt, make three.

Ch 4, 3 hdc into 3rd ch from hook, 3 hdc into last, ch 2, sl st into same st. Fasten off and leave a long tail for sewing. Sew the frills onto the front loops of the shirt in line with the nose. Sew the first frill onto the front loops of round 3, the second onto round 2, and the last onto round 1. Weave in the ends.

EYEBROWS, NOSE, AND MUSTACHE

Using black thread, embroider the eyebrows between rounds 13 and 15. With skin-colored yarn, embroider the nose between rounds 18 and 19. Mark the position of the mustache with four pins. Place two pins next to each other below the nose between rounds 19 and 20. Place two more pins one round below and two stitches away from the previous pins. Using black thread, embroider a thin line between the two sets of pins.

COAT

Use the color of the coat. Work in rows, turning at the end of each row. Ch 1 at the beginning does not count as sc.

Row 1. Ch 19, sc into 2nd ch from hook and next 17, turn (18).

Row 2. Ch 1, sc, {inc, sc into 4} 3 times, inc, sc into last, turn (22).

Row 3. Ch 1, sc into each, turn (22).

Row 4. Ch 1, sc, {inc, sc into 5} 3 times, inc, sc into last 2, turn (26).

Row 5. Ch 1, sc into each, turn (26).

Row 6. Ch 1, sc into 2, {inc, sc into 3} 6 times, turn (32).

Rows 7–11. Ch 1, sc into each, turn (32).

Row 12. Ch 1, sc into 2, {inc, sc into 6} 4 times, inc, sc into last, turn (37).

Rows 13–18. Ch 1, sc into each, turn (37).

Row 19. Ch 1, twisted sc (see here) into each (37). Place the coat in front of you with the right side facing out. Join the purple yarn with a sl st to the very first row of the coat, and crochet twisted sc into each st. Fasten off and leave a long tail for sewing. Fold the upper part of the coat to form a collar and place the coat on the doll. Secure it with pins and stitch it onto the body on both sides next to the shirt frills.

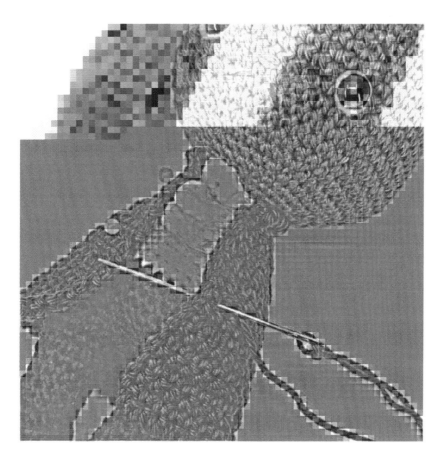

ARMS

Start with the skin color, make two.

Rnd 1. 6 sc into magic ring (6).

Rnd 2. {sc, inc} 3 times (9).

Rnd 3. Sc into each (9).

Rnd 4. {sc into 2, dec} 2 times, sc into last (7).

Rnd 5. Sc into each (7).

Change to the color of the coat.

Rnd 6. Sc into each BLO (7).

Rnds 7–12. Sc into each (7).

Fasten off and leave a long tail for sewing.

SHIRT CUFFS

Use the color of the shirt, make two.

Join with a sl st to a front loop of round 5 of the arm. Ch 2, 2 dc into same front loop, 3 dc into each of next 6 front loops, join with a sl st to first dc. Fasten off and weave in the ends. Position an arm on each side of the doll and sew them into place.

HAIR

Use the hair color and a piece of yarn or a stitch marker for marking the rounds as you are crocheting the main part of the hair. Leave the marker in place because you will need it when you are crocheting the curls.

Rnd 1. 6 sc into magic ring (6).

Rnd 2. 2 sc in each st (12).

Rnd 3. {sc, inc} 6 times BLO (18).

Rnd 4. {sc into 2, inc} 6 times (24).

Rnd 5. {sc into 3, inc} 6 times BLO (30).

Rnd 6. {sc into 4, inc} 6 times (36).

Rnd 7. {sc into 5, inc} 6 times BLO (42).

Rnd 8. {sc into 6, inc} 6 times (48).

Rnd 9. {sc into 7, inc} 6 times BLO (54).

Rnd 10. Sc into each (54).

Rnd 11. Sc into each BLO (54).

Rnd 12. Sc into each (54).

Rnd 13. Sc into each BLO (54).

Rnd 14. Sc into each (54).

Rnd 15. Sc into each BLO (54).

Rnd 16. Sc into each (54).

Rnd 17. Sc into each BLO (54).

Rnd 18. Sc into each (54).

Rnd 19. Sc into each BLO (54).

Do not fasten off. You will now crochet the curls by working into the front loops of rounds 18 to 2 of the hair.

CURLS

Front loops of Rnd 18: Ch 1, sl st into first front loop, ch 9, sc into 2nd ch from hook, {inc, sc} 3 times, inc into last. Sl st into next 3 front loops on the wig.

Ch 11, sc into 2nd ch from hook, {inc, sc} 4 times, inc into last. Sl st into next 3 front loops on the wig.

Ch 13, sc into 2nd ch from hook, {inc, sc} 5 times, inc into last. Sl st into next 3 front loops on the wig.

Ch 11, sc into 2nd ch from hook, {inc, sc} 4 times, inc into last. Sl st into next 3 front loops on the wig.

Ch 9, sc into 2nd ch from hook, {inc, sc} 3 times, inc into last. Sl st into next 3 front loops on the wig.

[Ch 7, sc into 2nd ch from hook, {inc, sc} 2 times, inc into last. Sl st into next 3 front loops on the wig] 3 times.

Ch 11, sc into 2nd ch from hook, {inc, sc} 4 times, inc into last. Sl st into next 3 front loops on the wig.

[Ch 9, sc into 2nd ch from hook, {inc, sc} 3 times, inc into last. Sl st into next 3 front loops on the wig] 3 times.

Ch 11, sc into 2nd ch from hook, {inc, sc} 4 times, inc into last. Sl st into next 3 front loops on the wig.

[Ch 7, sc into 2nd ch from hook, {inc, sc} 2 times, inc into last. Sl st into next 3 front loops on the wig] 4 times. Sl st into last 4 front loops on the wig (17 curls).

Front loops of Rnd 16: Sl st into first 2 front loops, ch 11, sc into 2nd ch from hook, {inc, sc} 4 times, inc into last. Sl st into next 3 front loops on the wig.

Ch 13, sc into 2nd ch from hook, {inc, sc} 5 times, inc into last. Sl st into next 3 front loops on the wig.

[Ch 15, sc into 2nd ch from hook, {inc, sc} 6 times, inc into last. Sl st into next 3 front loops on the wig] 2 times.

Ch 11, sc into 2nd ch from hook, {inc, sc} 4 times, inc into last. Sl st into next 3 front loops on the wig.

[Ch 7, sc into 2nd ch from hook, {inc, sc} 2 times, inc into last. Sl st into next 3 front loops on the wig] 3 times.

Ch 11, sc into 2nd ch from hook, {inc, sc} 4 times, inc into last. Sl st into next 3 front loops on the wig.

[Ch 9, sc into 2nd ch from hook, {inc, sc} 3 times, inc into last. Sl st into next 3 front loops on the wig] 3 times.

Ch 11, sc into 2nd ch from hook, {inc, sc} 4 times, inc into last. Sl st into next 3 front loops on the wig.

[Ch 7, sc into 2nd ch from hook, {inc, sc} 2 times, inc into last. Sl st into next 3 front loops on the wig] 4 times. Sl st into last 4 front loops on the wig (17 curls).

Front loops of Rnd 14: Repeat Rnd 16.

Front loops of Rnd 12: Sl st into first 2 front loops, ch 11, sc into 2nd ch from hook, {inc, sc} 4 times, inc into last. Sl st into next 3 front loops on the wig.

[Ch 13, sc into 2nd ch from hook, {inc, sc} 5 times, inc into last. Sl st into next 3 front loops on the wig] 3 times.

Ch 9, sc into 2nd ch from hook, {inc, sc} 3 times, inc into last. Sl st into next 3 front loops on the wig.

[Ch 7, sc into 2nd ch from hook, {inc, sc} 2 times, inc into last. Sl st into next 3 front loops on the wig] 3 times.

[Ch 9, sc into 2nd ch from hook, {inc, sc} 3 times, inc into last. Sl st into next 3 front loops on the wig] 5 times.

[Ch 7, sc into 2nd ch from hook, {inc, sc} 2 times, inc into last. Sl st into next 3 front loops on the wig] 4 times.

Sl st into last 4 front loops on the wig (17 curls).

Front loops of Rnd 10: Repeat Rnd 12.

Front loops of Rnd 8: Sl st into first front loop, [ch 11, sc into 2nd ch from hook, {inc, sc} 4 times, inc into last. Sl st into next 3 front loops on the wig] 3 times.

Ch 9, sc into 2nd ch from hook, {inc, sc} 3 times, inc into last. Sl st into next 3 front loops on the wig.

[Ch 7, sc into 2nd ch from hook, {inc, sc} 2 times, inc into last. Sl st into next 3 front loops on the wig] 10 times. Sl st into last 5 front loops on the wig (14 curls).

Front loops of Rnd 6: Sl st into first front loop, [ch 9, sc into 2nd ch from hook, {inc, sc} 3 times, inc into last. Sl st into next 3 front loops on the wig] 3 times.

[Ch 7, sc into 2nd ch from hook, {inc, sc} 2 times, inc into last. Sl st into next 3 front loops on the wig] 8 times. Sl st into last 5 front loops on the wig (14 curls).

Front loops of Rnd 4: Sl st into the first front loop, [ch 7, sc into 2nd ch from hook, {inc, sc} 2 times, inc into last. Sl st into next 3 front loops on the wig] 7 times. Sl st into last 5 front loops on the wig (7 curls).

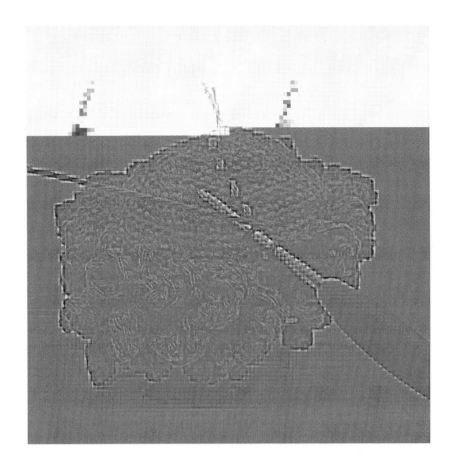

Front loops of Rnd 2: Sl st into first front loop, [ch 7, sc into 2nd ch from hook, {inc, sc} 2 times, inc into last. Sl st into next 3 front loops on the wig] 4 times. Sl st into last 5 front loops on the wig (4 curls).

Fasten off and leave a long tail for sewing. Place the hair on the head, secure it with pins, and sew it into place.

KATHERINE JOHNSON

Katherine Johnson was an American mathematician. She graduated summa cum laude from college at the age of eighteen with degrees in mathematics and French. She became a teacher, but left the profession to start a family. When her three daughters were older, she became one of the first African-American women to work as a NASA scientist. She helped to make it possible for John Glenn to be the first American to orbit the Earth. And in 1969 she calculated the precise trajectories that would allow Apollo 11—with Neil Armstrong on board— to land on the Moon and safely return to Earth.

MATERIALS

B-1 or C-2 (2.5 mm) crochet hook

$5/16$" (8 mm) safety eyes

Tapestry needle

Polyester fiberfill

Black thread for embroidery

Small amount of white felt

18 gauge (1 mm) floral stem wire

Round-nose pliers

YARNS

Scheepjes Catona 100% cotton yarn:

507 Chocolate—skin, 22 g

510 Sky Blue—dress, 25 g

106 Snow White—stripes on dress, 4 g

110 Jet Black—hair, 20 g

248 Champagne—shoes, 3 g

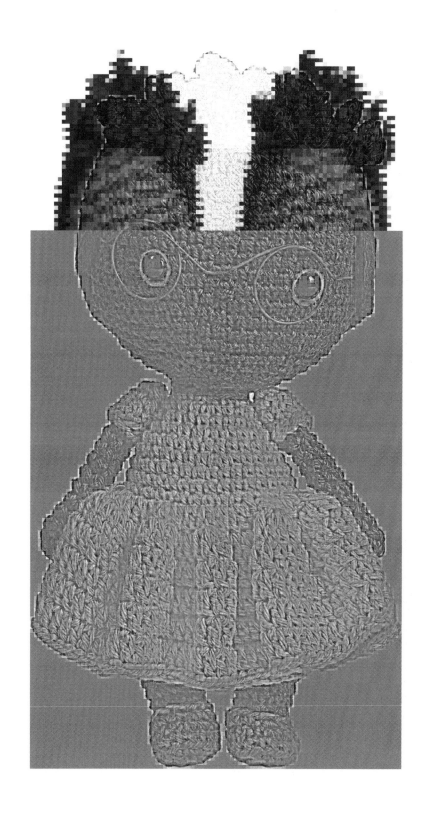

HEAD

Start with the skin color.

Rnd 1. 6 sc into magic ring (6).

Rnd 2. 2 sc into each (12).

Rnd 3. {sc, inc} 6 times (18).

Rnd 4. {sc into 2, inc} 6 times (24).

Rnd 5. {sc into 3, inc} 6 times (30).

Rnd 6. {sc into 4, inc} 6 times (36).

Rnd 7. {sc into 5, inc} 6 times (42).

Rnd 8. {sc into 6, inc} 6 times (48).

Rnd 9. {sc into 7, inc} 6 times (54).

Rnds 10–16. Sc into each (54).

Rnd 17. {sc into 8, inc} 6 times (60).

Rnds 18–20. Sc into each (60).

Rnd 21. {sc into 8, dec} 6 times (54).

Rnd 22. {sc into 7, dec} 6 times (48).

Rnd 23. {sc into 6, dec} 6 times (42).

Rnd 24. {sc into 5, dec} 6 times (36).

Add the eyes (see here for guidance).

Rnd 25. {sc into 4, dec} 6 times (30).

Rnd 26. {sc into 3, dec} 6 times (24).

Start to stuff the head.

Rnd 27. {sc into 2, dec} 6 times (18).

Rnd 28. {sc, dec} 6 times (12).

Continue to stuff the head firmly.

Rnd 29. Sc into each FLO (12).

Change to the color of the dress.

BODY

Rnd 1. {sc, inc} 6 times (18).

Rnd 2. {sc into 2, inc} 6 times (24).

Rnd 3. Sc into each (24).

Rnd 4. {sc into 3, inc} 6 times (30).

Rnd 5. Sc into each (30).

Rnd 6. {sc into 4, inc} 6 times (36).

Rnd 7. Sc into each (36).

Rnd 8. Sc into each (36).

Rnd 9. Sc into each (36).

Change to the skin color.

Rnd 10. Sc into each BLO (36).

Rnds 11–12. Sc into each (36).

Rnd 13. {sc into 16, dec} 2 times (34).

Rnds 14–15. Sc into each (34).

Do not fasten off, continue with the legs. Stuff the neck and body continuously.

LEGS

To make the legs, divide the work: 14 stitches for each of the legs, and 3 stitches between the legs, both front and back. Mark the stitches with yarn or a stitch marker. Make sure the legs line up with the eyes. If the last stitch of the body is within the 14 stitches for the legs, then continue crocheting. If it is within the 3 stitches, then fasten off, leave a tail for sewing later, and rejoin the skin-colored yarn with a sl st at the back of the doll.

Rnds 1–3. Sc into each (14).

Rnd 4. {sc into 5, dec} 2 times (12).

Rnds 5–8. Sc into each (12).

Stuff the body firmly and stuff the leg as you crochet it.

Rnd 9. {sc into 4, dec} 2 times (10).

Rnds 10–12. Sc into each (10).

Stuff the leg firmly.

Rnd 13. Dec 5 times (5).

Fasten off, sew up the small hole, and weave in the ends. For the second leg, rejoin with a sl st at the back of the doll and work the leg. When finished, sew up the hole between the legs. Weave in the ends.

SKIRT

Using the color of the dress, join with a sl st to a front loop of round 9 at the center back of the body. Work continuously, but join with a sl st at the end of each round. Ch 2 at the beginning does not count as dc.

Rnd 1. Ch 2, 2 dc into each (72).

Rnd 2. Ch 2, 2 dc into each (144).

Rnds 3–6. Ch 2, dc into each (144).

Change to white yarn for the stripe around the hem of the skirt. Turn the doll upside down and crochet slip stitches into the last round from the wrong side of the skirt. Fasten off and weave in the ends.

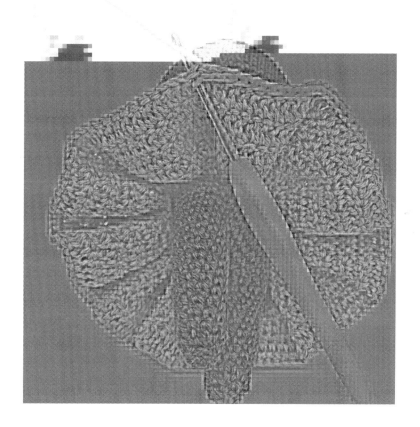

EYEBROWS AND NOSE

Using black thread, embroider the eyebrows between rounds 12 and 14. With skin-colored yarn, embroider the nose between rounds 18 and 19.

ARMS

Use the skin color, make two.

Rnd 1. 6 sc into magic ring (6).

Rnd 2. {sc, inc} 3 times (9).

Rnd 3. Sc into each (9).

Rnd 4. {sc into 1, dec} 3 times (6).

Rnds 5–12. Sc into each (6).

Fasten off and leave a long tail for sewing. Sew up the hole and weave in the ends.

SHIRT SLEEVES

Use the color of the dress, make two.

Rnd 1. 6 sc into magic ring (6).

Rnd 2. {sc, inc} 3 times (9).

Rnds 3–4. Sc into each (9).

Change to white yarn and crochet slip stitches into the last round from the wrong side of the sleeve. Fasten off and leave a long tail for sewing. Place the arms into the sleeves. Using small stitches, sew the sleeves onto the arms. Sew the sleeved arms onto the body. Weave in the ends.

SHOES

Use the color of the shoes, make two.

Rnd 1. Ch 4, 2 sc into 2nd ch from hook, sc, 3 sc into next. Continue working on the other side of the foundation chain: sc, 2 sc into last (9).

Rnd 2. Inc 2 times, sc, inc 3 times, sc, inc 2 times (16).

Rnd 3. Sc into each BLO (16).

Rnd 4. Sc into 5, dec 3 times, sc into 5 (13).

Rnd 5. Sc into 6, dec, sc into 5 (12).

Fasten off and leave a long tail for sewing. Add stuffing to the toe of the shoes, position them on the legs, and sew them into place. Weave in the ends.

HAIR

Use the hair color.

Rnd 1. 6 sc into magic ring (6).

Rnd 2. 2 sc into each (12).

Rnd 3. {sc, inc} 6 times (18).

Rnd 4. {sc into 2, inc} 6 times (24).

Rnd 5. {sc into 3, inc} 6 times (30).

Rnd 6. {sc into 4, inc} 6 times (36).

Rnd 7. {sc into 5, inc} 6 times (42).

Rnd 8. {sc into 6, inc} 6 times (48).

Rnd 9. {sc into 7, inc} 6 times (54).

Rnds 10–15. Sc into each (54).

Rnd 16. Sc, 3 hdc into next, sc into 25, 3 hdc into next, sc into 26 (58).

Rnd 17. Sc into 2, 3 hdc into next, sc into 27, 3 hdc into next, sc into 27 (62).

Rnd 18. Hdc into next 3, 3 hdc into next, sc into 29, 3 hdc into next, hdc into 28 (66).

Rnd 19. Hdc into 4, 3 hdc into next, sc into 9, sl st into next, and continue with the curls:

* Ch 10, sc into 2nd ch from hook, {inc, sc into next} 4 times, inc into last. Sl st into next 2 on the hair. Repeat from * 6 times. For the last curl, crochet only one sl st on the hair. Continue on the hair:

Sc into 8, 3 hdc into next, hdc into 29. Join with sl st into first st of round 19.

Fasten off and leave a long tail for sewing. Place the hair on the head, secure it with pins, and sew it into place.

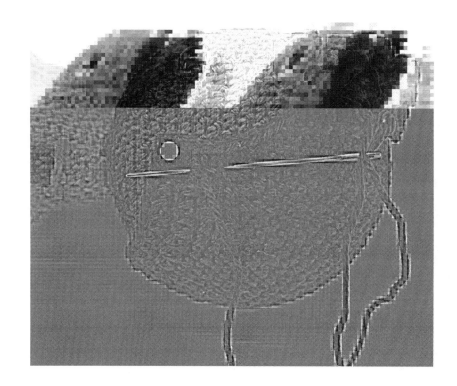

GLASSES

Take the floral wire and find a round object to use to form the ring shape for the glasses. I used the plastic part of a thread spool, with a ¾" (2 cm) diameter. Wrap the longer end of the wire around the spool, leaving 1½" (4 cm) on the shorter end. Wrap the wire all the way around the spool. For the other ring of the glasses, measure 1¾" (4.5 cm) from the first ring on the longer end of the wire and wrap it around the spool again. Use the spool to shape the curved bridge of the glasses. Bend the stems at right angles and place the glasses on the doll. Insert the stems into the head four stitches away from the eyes between rounds 16 and 17, below the hair.

ABRAHAM LINCOLN

Abraham Lincoln was the sixteenth president of the United States of America. He served as president for five years, until his assassination in 1865. He was self-educated, and though he was born in poverty, he became a successful lawyer, Illinois state legislator, and a US congressman. As a president he is best known for leading the country during the Civil War and keeping the country united. He also pushed to end slavery by issuing the Emancipation Proclamation and, later, the Thirteenth Amendment, which outlawed slavery and freed all slaves in the United States.

MATERIALS

B-1 or C-2 (2.5mm) crochet hook

$^5/_{16}$" (8 mm) safety eyes

Tapestry needle

Polyester fiberfill

Black thread for embroidery

Small amount of white felt

YARNS

Scheepjes Catona 100% cotton yarn:

130 Old Lace—skin, 20 g

106 Snow White—shirt, 10 g

074 Mercury—pants, 10 g

110 Jet Black—hat, coat, shoes, 35 g

507 Chocolate—hair, 18 g

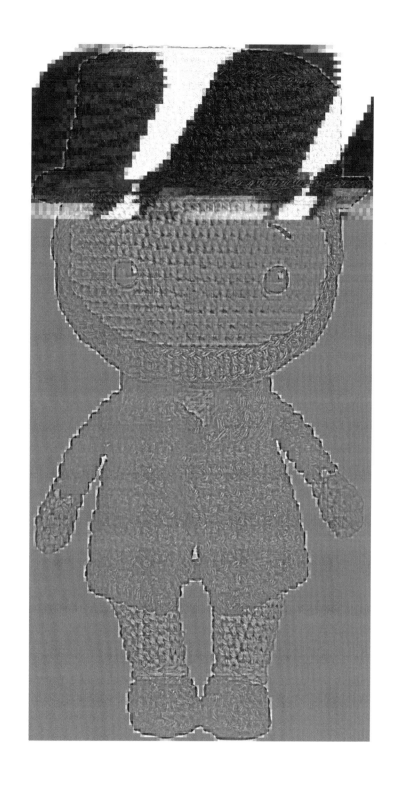

HEAD

Start with the skin color.

Rnd 1. 6 sc into magic ring (6).

Rnd 2. 2 sc into each (12).

Rnd 3. {sc, inc} 6 times (18).

Rnd 4. {sc into 2, inc} 6 times (24).

Rnd 5. {sc into 3, inc} 6 times (30).

Rnd 6. {sc into 4, inc} 6 times (36).

Rnd 7. {sc into 5, inc} 6 times (42).

Rnd 8. {sc into 6, inc} 6 times (48).

Rnd 9. {sc into 7, inc} 6 times (54).

Rnds 10–16. Sc into each (54).

Rnd 17. {sc into 8, inc} 6 times (60).

Rnds 18–20. Sc into each (60).

Rnd 21. {sc into 8, dec} 6 times (54).

Rnd 22. {sc into 7, dec} 6 times (48).

Rnd 23. {sc into 6, dec} 6 times (42).

Rnd 24. {sc into 5, dec} 6 times (36).

Add the eyes (see here for guidance).

Rnd 25. {sc into 4, dec} 6 times (30).

Rnd 26. {sc into 3, dec} 6 times (24).

Start to stuff the head.

Rnd 27. {sc into 2, dec} 6 times (18).

Rnd 28. {sc, dec} 6 times (12).

Continue to stuff the head firmly.

Rnd 29. Sc into each FLO (12).

Change to the color of the shirt.

BODY

Rnd 1. {sc, inc} 6 times (18).

Rnd 2. BLO {sc into 2, inc} 6 times (24).

Rnd 3. BLO sc into each (24).

Rnd 4. BLO {sc into 3, inc} 6 times (30).

Rnd 5. BLO sc into each (30).

Rnd 6. BLO {sc into 4, inc} 6 times (36).

Rnd 7. BLO sc into each (36).

Rnd 8. BLO sc into each (36).

Rnd 9. BLO sc into each (36).

Change to the color of the pants.

Rnd 10. Sc into each BLO (36).

Rnds 11–12. Sc into each (36).

Rnd 13. {sc into 16, dec} 2 times (34).

Rnds 14–15. Sc into each (34).

Do not fasten off, continue with the legs. Stuff the neck and body continuously.

LEGS

To make the legs, divide the work: 14 stitches for each of the legs, and 3 stitches between the legs, both front and back. Mark the stitches with yarn or a stitch marker. Make sure the legs line up with the eyes. If the last stitch of the body is within the 14 stitches for the legs, then continue crocheting. If it is within the 3 stitches, then fasten off, leave a tail for sewing later, and rejoin the pants-colored yarn with a sl st at the back of the doll.

Rnds 1–3. Sc into each (14).

Rnd 4. {sc into 5, dec} 2 times (12).

Rnds 5–8. Sc into each (12).

Stuff the body firmly and stuff the leg as you crochet it.

Rnd 9. {sc into 4, dec} 2 times (10).

Change to the skin color.

Rnd 10. Sc into each BLO (10).

Rnds 11–12. Sc into each (10).

Stuff the leg firmly.

Rnd 13. Dec 5 times (5).

Fasten off, sew up the small hole, and weave in the ends. For the second leg, rejoin with a sl st at the back of the doll and work the leg. When finished, sew up the hole between the legs. Weave in the ends. With the color of the pants, rejoin with a sl st in the front loop of round 9 at the back of the leg. Crochet slip stitches into each front loop. Fasten off and weave in the ends.

EYEBROWS AND NOSE

Using black thread, embroider the eyebrows between rounds 13 and 15. With skin-colored yarn, embroider the nose between rounds 18 and 19.

SHOES

Use the color of the shoes, make two.

Rnd 1. Ch 4, 2 sc into 2nd ch from hook, sc, 3 sc into next. Continue working on the other side of the foundation chain: sc, 2 sc into last (9).

Rnd 2. Inc 2 times, sc, inc 3 times, sc, inc 2 times (16).

Rnd 3. Sc into each BLO (16).

Rnd 4. Sc into 5, dec 3 times, sc into 5 (13).

Rnd 5. Sc into 6, dec, sc into 5 (12).

Fasten off and leave a long tail for sewing. Add stuffing to the toe of the shoes, position them on the legs, and sew them into place. Weave in the ends.

COAT

Use the color of the coat.

Work in rows, turning at the end of each row. Ch 1 at the beginning does not count as sc.

Row 1. Ch 21, sc into 2nd ch from hook and next 19, turn (20).

Row 2. Ch 1, sc into 2, {inc, sc into 4} 3 times, inc, sc into 2, turn (24).

Row 3. Ch 1, sc into each, turn (24).

Row 4. Sc into 2, {inc, sc into 5} 3 times, inc, sc into 3, turn (28).

Row 5. Sc into each, turn (28).

Row 6. Sc, {inc, sc into 4} 5 times, inc, sc into last, turn (34).

Rows 7–18. Sc into each, turn (34).

Row 19. Twisted sc (see here) into each (49).

Fasten off and weave in the ends. Fold the upper part of the coat to form a collar and place it onto the body of the doll. Cross the edges of the coat on the belly of the doll. Secure it with pins and sew it to the body.

ARMS

Start with the skin color, make two.

Rnd 1. 6 sc into magic ring (6).

Rnd 2. {sc, inc} 3 times (9).

Rnd 3. Sc into each (9).

Rnd 4. {sc into 2, dec} 2 times, sc into last (7).

Change to the color of the coat.

Rnds 5–12. Sc into each (7).

Fasten off and leave a long tail for sewing. Position an arm on each side of the doll and sew them into place.

BEARD

Use the hair color and work in rows.

Row 1. Ch 30, hdc into 3rd ch from hook and next 7, dc into next 12, hdc into next 8, turn. (28).

Row 2. Ch 1, {sc, inc} 4 times, hdc into next 12, {inc, sc} 4 times (36).

Fasten off and leave a long tail for sewing. Place the ends of the beard between rounds 15 and 16 on both sides of the head. The upper part of the beard should be between rounds 22 and 23. Sew it onto the face by the upper edge of the beard.

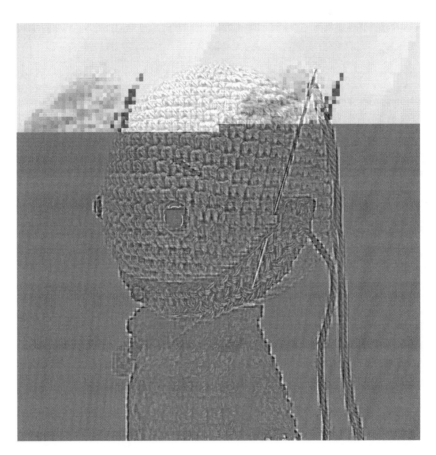

HAIR

Use the hair color.

Rnd 1. 6 sc into magic ring (6).

Rnd 2. 2 sc into each (12).

Rnd 3. {sc, inc} 6 times (18).

Rnd 4. {sc into 2, inc} 6 times (24).

Rnd 5. {sc into 3, inc} 6 times (30).

Rnd 6. {sc into 4, inc} 6 times (36).

Rnd 7. {sc into 5, inc} 6 times (42).

Rnd 8. {sc into 6, inc} 6 times (48).

Rnd 9. {sc into 7, inc} 6 times (54).

Rnds 10–17. Sc into each (54).

Rnd 18. Sl st into 2, hdc into next 2, dc into next 48, hdc into next, sc into last (54). Join with a sl st to first st of round 18.

Fasten off and leave a long tail for sewing. Place the hair on the head, making sure that the hair covers the ends of the beard. Secure it with pins and sew it into place.

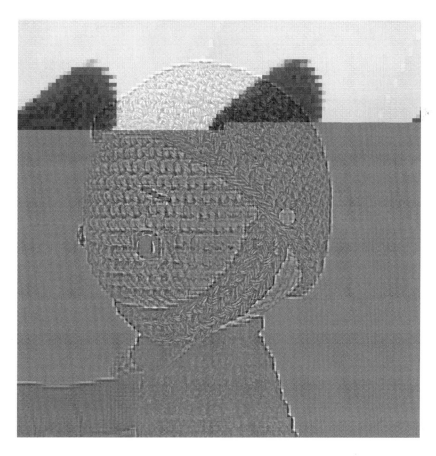

HAT

Use the color of the hat.

Rnd 1. 7 sc into magic ring (7).

Rnd 2. 2 sc into each (14).

Rnd 3. {sc, inc} 7 times (21).

Rnd 4. {sc into 2, inc} 7 times (28).

Rnd 5. {sc into 3, inc} 7 times (35).

Rnd 6. {sc into 4, inc} 7 times (42).

Rnd 7. {sc into 5, inc} 7 times (49).

Rnd 8. {sc into 6, inc} 7 times (56).

Rnd 9. {sc into 7, inc} 7 times (63).

Rnd 10. Sc into each (63).

Rnd 11. Sc into each BLO (63).

Rnds 12–18. Sc into each (63).

Rnd 19. Sc into each (63). Join with a sl st to first st.

Rnd 20. Ch 2, FLO {dc into 2, inc} 21 times (84). Join with a sl st into first st.

Rnd 21. Sl st into each. (84)

Fasten off and weave in the ends. Add stuffing to the hat, place it on the head, and sew it into place.

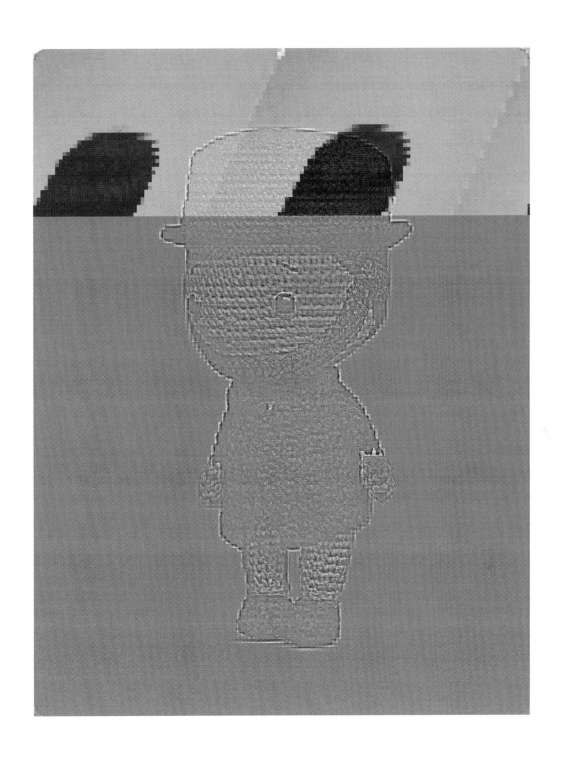

PABLO PICASSO

Pablo Picasso was a prolific Spanish painter and sculptor—undoubtedly one of the most influential artists of the twentieth century. Besides his more than twenty thousand paintings, drawings, sculptures, and ceramics, he is also known for cofounding the Cubist art movement and for the coinvention of collage. His undisputed talent, eccentric style, and free spirit made him the father of modern art.

MATERIALS

B-1 or C-2 (2.5 mm) crochet hook

$5/16$" (8 mm) safety eyes

Tapestry needle

Polyester fiberfill

Black thread for embroidery

Small amount of white felt

YARNS

Scheepjes Catona 100% cotton yarn:

505 Linen—skin, 20 g

106 Snow White—shirt, 5 g

110 Jet Black—shirt, shoes, 8 g

503 Hazelnut—pants, 10 g

Scheepjes Softly yarn:

494 White—hair, 8 g

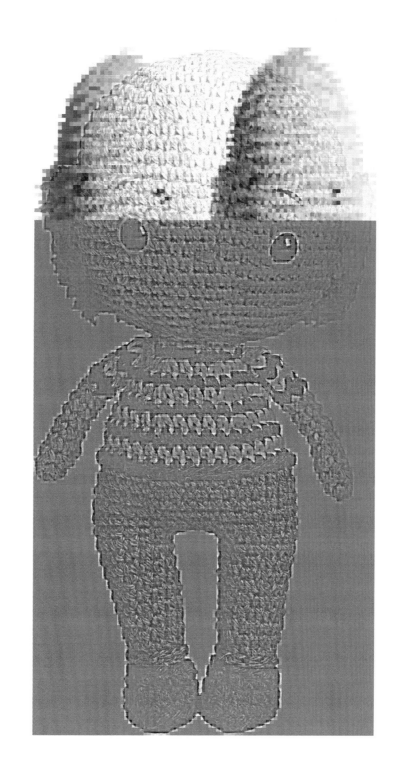

HEAD

Start with the skin color.

Rnd 1. 6 sc into magic ring (6).

Rnd 2. 2 sc into each (12).

Rnd 3. {sc, inc} 6 times (18).

Rnd 4. {sc into 2, inc} 6 times (24).

Rnd 5. {sc into 3, inc} 6 times (30).

Rnd 6. {sc into 4, inc} 6 times (36).

Rnd 7. {sc into 5, inc} 6 times (42).

Rnd 8. {sc into 6, inc} 6 times (48).

Rnd 9. {sc into 7, inc} 6 times (54).

Rnds 10–15. Sc into each (54).

Rnd 16. Sc into 28 BLO, sc into 26 (54).

Rnd 17. {sc into 8, inc} 4 times, place stitch marker for first safety eye, {sc into 8, inc}, sc into next, place stitch marker for second safety eye, sc into 7, inc (60).

Rnd 18. Sc into 31 BLO, sc into 29 (60).

Rnd 19. Sc into each (60).

Rnd 20. Sc into 31 BLO, sc into 29 (60).

Rnd 21. {sc into 8, dec} 6 times (54).

Rnd 22. Sc into next, sc into 6 BLO, dec BLO, {sc into 7, dec} 2 times BLO, {sc into 7, dec} 3 times (48).

Rnd 23. {sc into 6, dec} 6 times (42).

Rnd 24. {sc into 5, dec} 6 times (36).

Add the eyes (see here for guidance).

Rnd 25. {sc into 4, dec} 6 times (30).

Rnd 26. {sc into 3, dec} 6 times (24).

Start to stuff the head.

Rnd 27. {sc into 2, dec} 6 times (18).

Rnd 28. {sc, dec} 6 times (12).

Continue to stuff the head firmly.

Rnd 29. Sc into each FLO (12).

Fasten off and weave in the ends.

HAIR

Use the hair color. Turn the head upside down, and * join with a sl st to the front loop of round 21 of the head. Crochet sc into each of the front loops of round 21.

After the last front loop, fasten off and weave in the ends. Repeat from * into the front loops of rounds 19, 17, and 15 of the head.

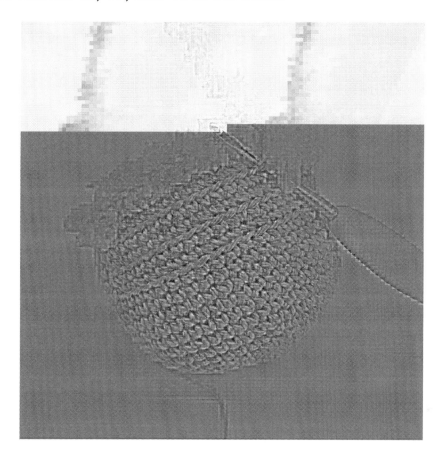

BODY

Start with the black shirt yarn. Join with a sl st to the center back of the neck. Work in continuous rounds but join with a sl st at the end of each round when you change colors. Ch 1 at the beginning does not count as sc.

Rnd 1. Ch 1, {sc, inc} 6 times (18). Change to the white shirt yarn.

Rnd 2. Ch 1, {sc into 2, inc} 6 times (24). Change to black.

Rnd 3. Ch 1, sc into each (24). Change to white.

Rnd 4. Ch 1, {sc into 3, inc} 6 times (30). Change to black.

Rnd 5. Ch 1, sc into each (30). Change to white.

Rnd 6. Ch 1, {sc into 4, inc} 6 times (36). Change to black.

Rnd 7. Ch 1, sc into each (36). Change to white.

Rnd 8. Ch 1, sc into each (36). Change to black, fasten off white.

Rnd 9. Ch 1, sc into each (36).

Change to the color of the trousers.

Rnd 10. Sc into each BLO (36).

Rnds 11–12. Sc into each (36).

Rnd 13. {sc into 16, dec} 2 times (34).

Rnds 14–15. Sc into each (34).

Do not fasten off, continue with the legs. Stuff the neck and body continuously.

LEGS

To make the legs, divide the work: 14 stitches for each of the legs, and 3 stitches between the legs, both front and back. Mark the stitches with yarn or a stitch marker. Make sure the legs line up with the eyes. If the last stitch of the body is within the 14 stitches for the legs, then continue crocheting. If it is within the 3 stitches, then fasten off, leave a tail for sewing later, and rejoin the pants-colored yarn with a sl st at the back of the doll.

Rnds 1–3. Sc into each (14).

Rnd 4. {sc into 5, dec} 2 times (12).

Rnds 5–8. Sc into each (12).

Stuff the body firmly and stuff the leg as you crochet it.

Rnd 9. {sc into 4, dec} 2 times (10).

Change to the skin color.

Rnd 10. Sc into each BLO (10).

Rnds 11–12. Sc into each (10).

Stuff the leg firmly.

Rnd 13. Dec 5 times (5).

Fasten off, sew up the small hole, and weave in the ends. For the second leg, rejoin with a sl st at the back of the doll and work the leg. When finished, sew up the hole between the legs. Weave in the ends.

PANT CUFFS

Use the color of the pants, make two.

Join with a sl st to the front loop of round 9 of the leg, sl st into each front loop. Fasten off and weave in the ends. Repeat for the second leg.

SHIRT EDGING

With black yarn, join with a slip stitch to the front loop of round 9 of the body, sl st into each front loop. Fasten off and weave in the ends.

EYEBROWS AND NOSE

Using black thread, embroider the eyebrows between rounds 13 and 15. With skin-colored yarn, embroider the nose between rounds 18 and 19.

ARMS

Start with the skin color, make two.

Rnd 1. 6 sc into magic ring (6).

Rnd 2. {sc, inc} 3 times (9).

Rnd 3. Sc into each (9).

Rnd 4. {sc into 2, dec} 2 times, sc into last (7).

Rnds 5–8. Sc into each (7). Change to black yarn.

Rnd 9. Sc into each (7). Change to white yarn.

Rnd 10. Sc into each (7). Change to black yarn.

Rnd 11. Sc into each (7). Change to white yarn.

Rnd 12. Sc into each (7).

Fasten off and leave a long tail for sewing. Position an arm on each side of the doll at round 2 of the body and sew them into place.

SHOES

Use the color of the shoes, make two.

Rnd 1. Ch 4, 2 sc into 2nd ch from hook, sc, 3 sc into next. Continue working on the other side of the foundation chain: sc, 2 sc into last (9).

Rnd 2. Inc 2 times, sc, inc 3 times, sc, inc 2 times (16).

Rnd 3. Sc into each BLO (16).

Rnd 4. Sc into 5, dec 3 times, sc into 5 (13).

Rnd 5. Sc into 6, dec, sc into 5 (12).

Fasten off and leave a long tail for sewing. Add stuffing to the toe of the shoes, position them on the legs, and sew them into place. Weave in the ends.

―――――

ROSA PARKS

Rosa Parks was an American activist in the civil rights movement. On December 1, 1955, she was arrested for refusing to give up her seat to a white passenger on a segregated bus in Montgomery, Alabama. Though she was not the first person to resist bus segregation, her brave move led to the Montgomery bus boycott, during which the black community refused to use the Montgomery buses for over a year. The boycott ended when the US Supreme Court ruled that bus segregation was unconstitutional. Parks later moved to Detroit and continued to fight to end racial injustice for the rest of her life.

MATERIALS

B-1 or C-2 (2.5 mm) crochet hook

$5/16$" (8 mm) safety eyes

Tapestry needle

Polyester fiberfill

Black thread for embroidery

Small amount of white felt

18 gauge (1 mm) floral stem wire

Round-nose pliers

YARNS

Scheepjes Catona 100% cotton yarn:

503 Hazelnut—skin, 22 g

106 Snow White—shirt, flower, 10 g

391 Deep Ocean Green—skirt, coat, 25 g

528 Silver Blue—suit edging, hat, 12 g

110 Jet Black—hair, 20 g

162 Black Coffee—shoes, 3 g

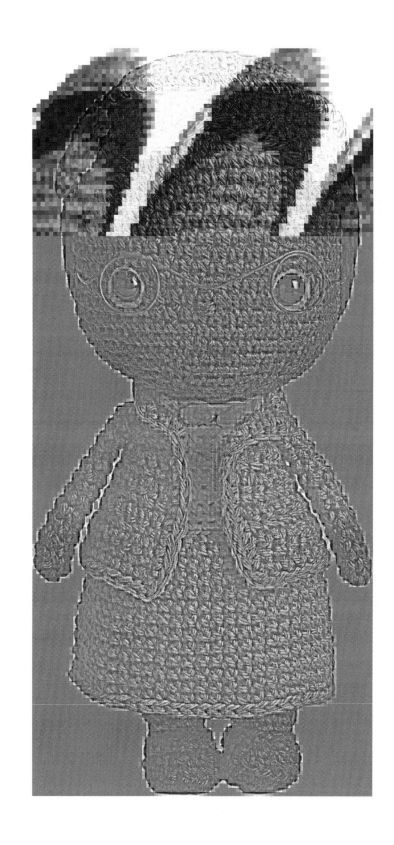

HEAD

Start with the skin color.

Rnd 1. 6 sc into magic ring (6).

Rnd 2. 2 sc into each (12).

Rnd 3. {sc, inc} 6 times (18).

Rnd 4. {sc into 2, inc} 6 times (24).

Rnd 5. {sc into 3, inc} 6 times (30).

Rnd 6. {sc into 4, inc} 6 times (36).

Rnd 7. {sc into 5, inc} 6 times (42).

Rnd 8. {sc into 6, inc} 6 times (48).

Rnd 9. {sc into 7, inc} 6 times (54).

Rnds 10–16. Sc into each (54).

Rnd 17. {sc into 8, inc} 6 times (60).

Rnds 18–20. Sc into each (60).

Rnd 21. {sc into 8, dec} 6 times (54).

Rnd 22. {sc into 7, dec} 6 times (48).

Rnd 23. {sc into 6, dec} 6 times (42).

Rnd 24. {sc into 5, dec} 6 times (36).

Add the eyes (see here for guidance).

Rnd 25. {sc into 4, dec} 6 times (30).

Rnd 26. {sc into 3, dec} 6 times (24).

Start to stuff the head.

Rnd 27. {sc into 2, dec} 6 times (18).

Rnd 28. {sc, dec} 6 times (12).

Continue to stuff the head firmly.

Rnd 29. Sc into each FLO (12).

Do not fasten off, continue with the body.

BODY

Rnd 1. {sc, inc} 6 times (18).

Change to the color of the shirt.

Rnd 2. BLO {sc into 2, inc} 6 times (24).

Rnd 3. BLO sc into each (24).

Rnd 4. BLO {sc into 3, inc} 6 times (30).

Rnd 5. BLO sc into each (30).

Rnd 6. BLO {sc into 4, inc} 6 times (36).

Rnd 7. BLO sc into each (36).

Rnd 8. BLO sc into each (36).

Change to the skin color, but before you continue, make the collar using the color of the shirt.

SHIRT COLLAR

Turn the doll upside down and join the white yarn with a sl st to a back loop of round 1 at the center back of the body. Work {(sc, dc, sc) into same st, sl st into next} 9 times. Fasten off and weave in the ends.

Continue crocheting the body:

Rnd 9. Sc into each BLO (36).

Rnds 10–12. Sc into each (36).

Rnd 13. {sc into 16, dec} 2 times (34).

Rnds 14–15. Sc into each (34).

Do not fasten off, continue with the legs. Stuff the neck and body continuously.

LEGS

To make the legs, divide the work: 14 stitches for each of the legs, and 3 stitches between the legs, both front and back. Mark the stitches with yarn or a stitch marker. Make sure the legs line up with the eyes. If the last stitch of the body is within the 14 stitches for the legs, then continue crocheting. If it is within the 3 stitches, then fasten off, leave a tail for sewing later, and rejoin the skin-colored yarn with a sl st at the back of the doll.

Rnds 1–3. Sc into each (14).

Rnd 4. {sc into 5, dec} 2 times (12).

Rnds 5–8. Sc into each (12).

Stuff the body firmly and stuff the leg as you crochet it.

Rnd 9. {sc into 4, dec} 2 times (10).

Rnds 10–12. Sc into each (10).

Stuff the leg firmly.

Rnd 13. Dec 5 times (5).

Fasten off, sew up the small hole, and weave in the ends. For the second leg, rejoin with a sl st at the back of the doll and work the leg. When finished, sew up the hole between the legs. Weave in the ends.

EYEBROWS AND NOSE

Using black thread, embroider the eyebrows between rounds 12 and 14. With skin-colored yarn, embroider the nose between rounds 18 and 19.

SKIRT

Use the light green yarn (to match the hat) for the contrast edging. Join with a sl st to a front loop of round 8 at the center back of the body. Work continuously, but join with a sl st at the end of each round. Ch 1 at the beginning does not count as sc. Work each sc in an "X" shape (see here) until the skirt is complete, or use standard sc if you prefer.

Rnd 1. Sl st into each (36). Change to dark green.

Rnd 2. Ch 1, sc into each BLO (36).

Rnd 3. Ch 1, {sc, inc} 18 times (54).

Rnds 4–14. Ch 1, sc into each (54).

Change to light green.

Rnd 15. Sl st into each.

Fasten off and weave in ends.

SHOES

Use the color of the shoes, make two.

Rnd 1. Ch 4, 2 sc into 2nd ch from hook, sc, 3 sc into next. Continue working on the other side of the foundation chain: sc, 2 sc into last (9).

Rnd 2. Inc 2 times, sc, inc 3 times, sc, inc 2 times (16).

Rnd 3. Sc into each BLO (16).

Rnd 4. Sc into 5, dec 3 times, sc into 5 (13).

Rnd 5. Sc into 6, dec, sc into 5 (12).

Fasten off and leave a long tail for sewing. Add stuffing to the toe of the shoes, position them on the legs, and sew them into place. Weave in the ends.

COAT

Start with the dark green yarn. Work in rows, turning at the end of each row. Ch 1 at the beginning does not count as sc.

Row 1. Ch 21, sc into 2nd ch from hook and next 19, turn (20).

Row 2. Ch 1, sc into 2, {inc, sc into 4} 3 times, inc, sc into 2, turn (24).

Row 3. Ch 1, sc into each, turn (24).

Row 4. Sc into 2, {inc, sc into 5} 3 times, inc, sc into 3, turn (28).

Row 5. Sc into each, turn (28).

Row 6. Sc, {inc, sc into 4} 5 times, inc, sc into last, turn (34).

Rows 7–9. Sc into each, turn (34).

Row 10. Sc, {inc, sc into 5} 5 times, inc, sc into 2, turn (40).

Rows 11–12. Sc into each, turn (40).

Change to light green.

Row 13. Sl st into each, turn (40).

Do not fasten off. Ch 1 and continue crocheting sc evenly up the front edge of the coat. Crochet 2 sc into the corner, then continue along the top of the coat. Crochet 2 sc into the other corner and then crochet sc evenly down the other front edge of the coat. Join with a sl st in the first st of row 13. Fasten off and weave in the ends. Fold the upper part of the coat to form a collar and place it onto the body of the doll. Secure it with pins and use small stitches on both sides to sew it into place.

ARMS

Start with the skin color, make two.

Rnd 1. 6 sc into magic ring (6).

Rnd 2. {sc, inc} 3 times (9).

Rnd 3. Sc into each (9).

Rnd 4. {sc into 2, dec} 2 times, sc into last (7).

Change to the dark green coat yarn.

Rnds 5–12. Sc into each (7).

Fasten off and leave a long tail for sewing. Position an arm on each side of the doll and sew them into place.

HAIR

Use the hair color.

Rnd 1. 6 sc into magic ring (6).

Rnd 2. 2 sc into each (12).

Rnd 3. {sc, inc} 6 times (18).

Rnd 4. {sc into 2, inc} 6 times (24).

Rnd 5. {sc into 3, inc} 6 times (30).

Rnd 6. {sc into 4, inc} 6 times (36).

Rnd 7. {sc into 5, inc} 6 times (42).

Rnd 8. {sc into 6, inc} 6 times (48).

Rnd 9. {sc into 7, inc} 6 times (54).

Rnds 10–17. Sc into each (54).

Rnd 18. Dc into 25, hdc into next, sl st into next 2, hdc into next, dc into last 25 (54).

Fasten off and leave a long tail for sewing. Place the hair on the head, secure it with pins, and sew it into place.

BUN

Use the hair color.

Rnd 1. Ch 4, 2 sc into 2nd ch from hook, sc, 3 sc into next. Continue working on the other side of the foundation chain: sc into last 2 (8).

Rnd 2. Inc 2 times, sc, inc 3 times, sc, inc (14).

Rnd 3. Inc 3 times, sc into 4, inc 3 times, sc into 4 (20).

Rnd 4. {sc, inc} 3 times, sc into 4, {sc, inc} 3 times, sc into 4 (26).

Rnd 5. Sc, {sc, inc} 3 times, sc into 7, {sc, inc} 3 times, sc into 6 (32).

Rnds 6–8. Sc into each (32).

Rnd 9. Sc into 6, sl st into next.

Fasten off and leave a long tail for sewing. Stuff the bun, then place it on the head between rounds 9 and 18 of the hair. Secure the bun with pins, stuff it, and sew it into place.

HAT

Use the light green hat color.

Rnd 1. 7 sc into magic ring (7).

Rnd 2. 2 sc into each (14).

Rnd 3. {sc, inc} 7 times (21).

Rnd 4. {sc into 2, inc} 7 times (28).

Rnd 5. {sc into 3, inc} 7 times (35).

Rnd 6. {sc into 4, inc} 7 times (42).

Rnd 7. Sc into each (42).

Rnd 8. Sc into each BLO (42).

Rnd 9. {sc into 5, inc} 7 times (49).

Rnds 10–11. Sc into each (49).

Rnd 12. Twisted sc (see here) into each (49).

Join with a sl st to the first st of round 12. Fasten off and weave in the ends. Place the hat on the hair above the bun. Secure it with a few stitches.

FLOWER

Use the flower color.

Rnd 1. 5 sc into magic ring (5). Join with sl st to first sc.

Rnd 2. {ch 1, 2 hdc into same st, ch 1, sl st into same st, sl st into next} 5 times.

Fasten off and leave a long tail for sewing. Sew the flower onto the right side of the hair.

GLASSES

Take the floral wire and find a round object to use to form the ring shape for the glasses. I used the plastic part of a thread spool, with a ½" (1.5 cm) diameter. Wrap the longer end of the wire around the spool, leaving 1½" (4 cm) on the shorter end. Wrap the wire all the way around the spool. For the other ring of the glasses, measure 1¾" (4.5 cm) from the first ring on the longer end of the wire and wrap it around the spool again. Use the spool to shape the curved bridge of the glasses. Bend the stems at right angles and place the glasses on the doll. Insert the stems into the head four stitches away from the eyes between rounds 16 and 17, below the hair.

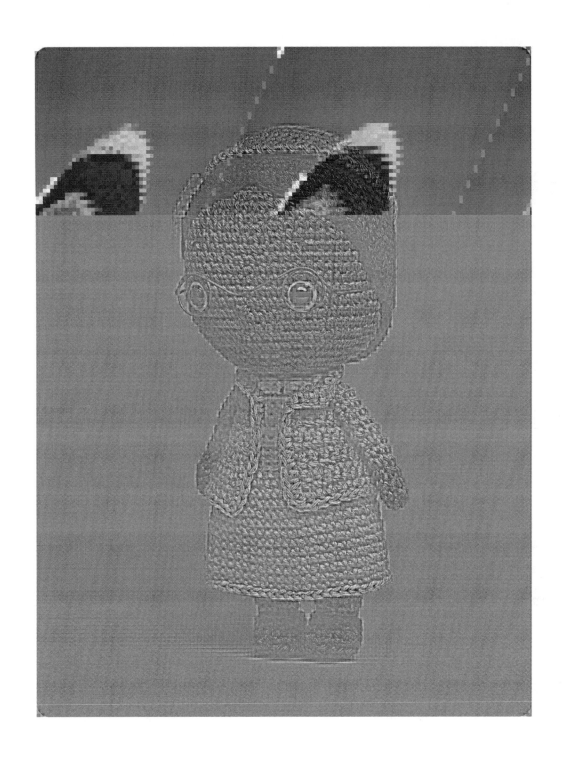

TECHNIQUES

Even experienced crocheters need to have their memories jogged from time to time. Whether you're a relative beginner or have been crocheting for years, these pages provide a handy reference guide for how to do the essential crochet stitches and techniques for the projects in this book.

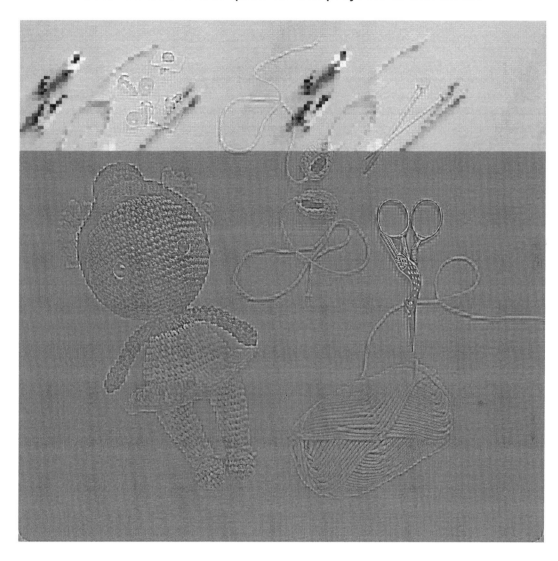

CROCHET ABBREVIATIONS

The abbreviations below are used throughout the patterns in the book:

BLO	back loop only
bpdc	back-post double crochet
ch	chain
dc	double crochet
dec	decrease(ing)
FLO	front loop only
fpdc	front-post double crochet
hdc	half double crochet
inc	increase(ing)
prev	previous
rnd(s)	round(s)
sc	single crochet
sk	skip
sl st(s)	slip stitch(es)
st(s)	stitch(es)

GAUGE AND PROJECT SIZING

For each of the projects, I used a 2.5 mm crochet hook, and Scheepjes Catona 100% Cotton Mercerized yarn in various colors. With this pairing, the sitting dolls are approximately 6 inches / 15 cm, and the standing ones are 7 inches / 18 cm tall.

If you prefer different yarn brands, feel free to crochet with those, but I suggest using 100% cotton yarn. With Catona yarn to give a 1" x 1" (2.5 cm x 2.5 cm) square, I crocheted 7 single crochet with 8 rounds. I achieved this gauge by crocheting in rounds.

Measurements will change depending on the hook size and yarn you use. If you use thicker yarn with a bigger crochet hook, the doll becomes taller. And the same way, if you use thinner yarn with a smaller crochet hook, the finished doll will be smaller.

STARTING AND FINISHING

Crochet can be worked in rows, beginning with a foundation chain, or in rounds, working outward from a foundation ring of chain stitches or a magic ring.

MAKING A SLIPKNOT

Almost every piece of crochet begins with a slipknot.

1. Make a yarn loop, as pictured.

2. Insert the crochet hook, as shown.

3. Gently pull on the short and long ends of yarn while holding the hook to create a slipknot.

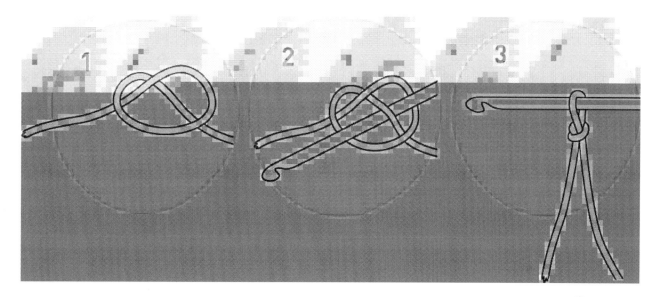

CHAIN STITCH (CH) / FOUNDATION CHAIN

1. Make a slipknot, as shown above. Holding the hook with the slipknot in your right hand and the yarn in your left hand, wrap the yarn over the hook and draw it through the loop.

2. This makes a new loop on the hook and completes the first chain stitch.

3. Repeat this process, drawing a new loop of yarn through the loop already on the hook until the foundation chain is the required length. Count each V-shaped loop on the front of the chain as one chain stitch, except for the loop on the hook, which is not counted.

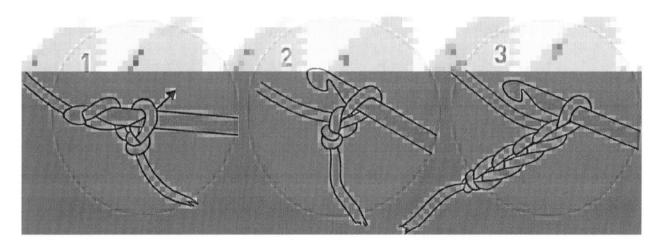

SLIP STITCH (SL ST)

1. Insert the hook in the designated stitch, wrap the yarn over the hook, and pull a new loop through both the work and the loop on the hook. One slip stitch (sl st) made.

2. Repeat Step 1 in each stitch to the end to complete one row of slip stitches.

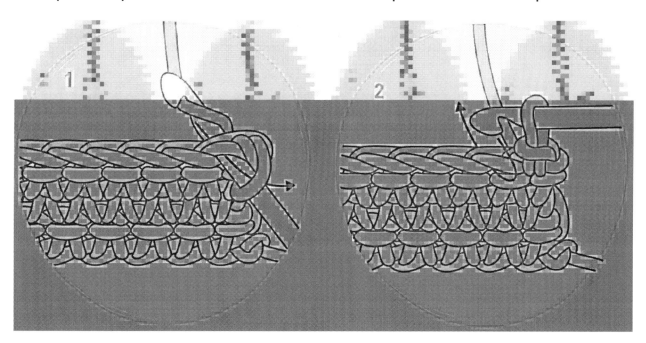

MAGIC RING

1. Start by making a loop in the yarn, as pictured. Insert the hook into the loop, following the direction of the arrow.

2. Hook the working yarn (the long end) and pull it through the loop, as pictured.

3. Make one chain stitch (or more, if directed by the pattern).

4. Crochet the desired number of stitches into the center of the loop.

5. Pull on the short yarn end to close the center of the magic ring.

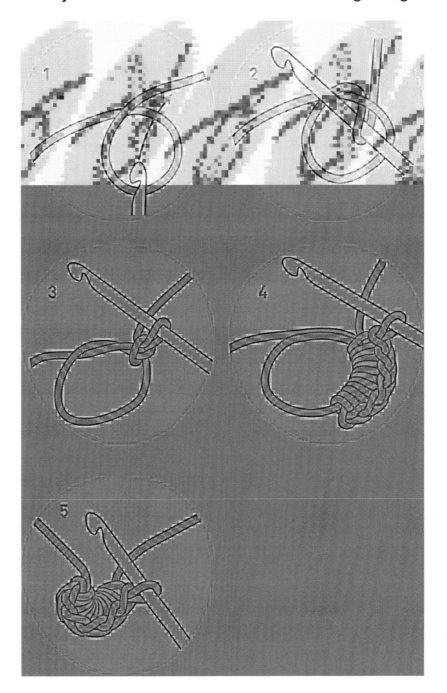

FOUNDATION RING

1. Work a short length of foundation chain as specified in the pattern. Join the chains into a ring by working a slip stitch into the first chain.

2. Work the first round of stitches into the center of the ring unless specified otherwise. At the end of the round, use a slip stitch to join the final stitch to the first stitch if instructed to do so in the pattern.

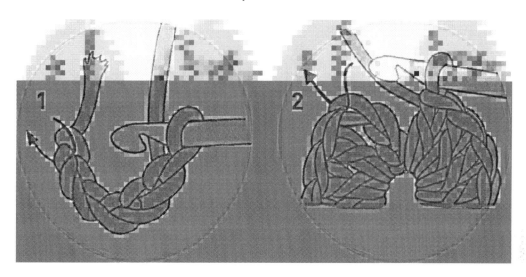

FASTENING OFF AND WEAVING IN ENDS

It is very easy to fasten off yarn when you have finished a piece of crochet, but do not cut the yarn too close to the work because you need enough yarn to weave in the end. It is important to weave in yarn ends securely so that they do not unravel. Do this as neatly as possible so that the woven yarn does not show through on the front of the work.

Fastening off

To fasten off the yarn securely, cut the yarn at least 4" (10 cm) away from the work, and pull the tail through the remaining loop on the hook, tightening it gently.

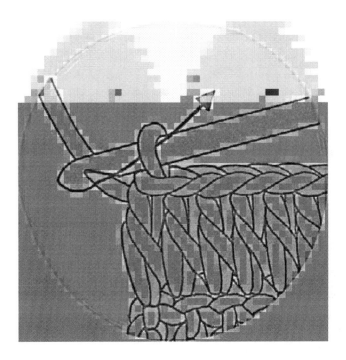

Weaving in yarn

To weave in a yarn end along the top or lower edge of a piece of crochet, start by threading the end into a yarn or tapestry needle. Take the needle through several stitches on the wrong side of the crochet, working stitch by stitch. Trim the remaining yarn.

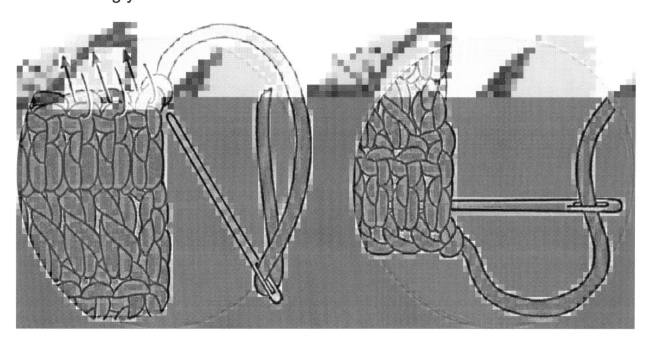

BASIC STITCHES

SINGLE CROCHET (SC)

1. Insert the hook in the designated stitch, wrap the yarn over the hook, and pull a new loop through this stitch only.

2. Wrap the yarn over the hook, and then pull a loop through both loops on the hook.

3. One loop remains on the hook. One single crochet stitch (sc) made. Repeat Steps 1–2 in each stitch to the end to complete one row of single crochet stitches.

HALF DOUBLE CROCHET (HDC)

1. Wrap the yarn over the hook and insert the hook in the designated stitch.

2. Pull a loop through this stitch. You now have three loops on the hook. Wrap the yarn over the hook again. Pull through all three loops on the hook.

3. One loop remains on the hook. One half double crochet stitch (hdc) made. Repeat Steps 1–2 in each stitch to the end to complete one row of half double crochet stitches.

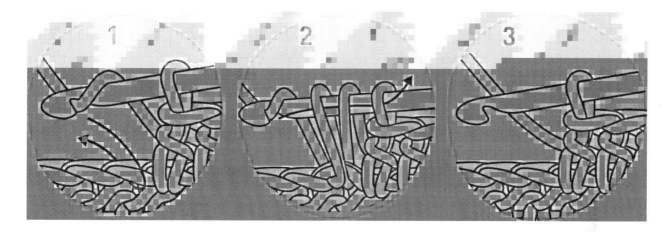

DOUBLE CROCHET (DC)

1. Wrap the yarn over the hook and insert the hook in the designated stitch.

2. Pull a loop through this stitch to make three loops on the hook. Wrap the yarn over the hook again. Pull a new loop through the first two loops on the hook, as pictured. Two loops remain on the hook. Wrap the yarn over the hook again. Pull a new loop through both remaining loops on the hook.

3. One double crochet stitch (dc) made. Repeat Steps 1–2 in each stitch to the end to complete one row of double crochet stitches.

BASIC STITCH VARIATIONS

SINGLE CROCHET (SC) IN AN "X" SHAPE

You can achieve this look if you wrap the yarn under the crochet hook instead of wrapping it over.

1. Insert the hook in the designated stitch. Wrap the yarn under the hook and pull a loop through to make two loops on the hook.

2. Wrap the yarn under the hook again and pull a loop through both loops on the hook. One loop remains on the hook. One single crochet in an "X" shape made.

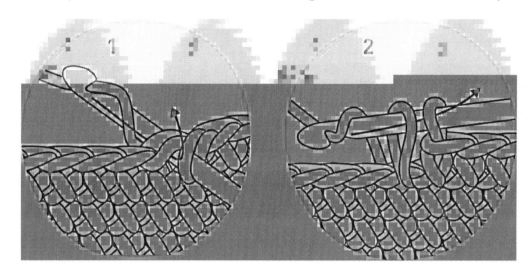

TWISTED SINGLE CROCHET

1. Insert the hook from front to back in the designated stitch. Wrap the yarn over the hook and pull a loop through the stitch to make two loops on the hook. Try to keep the loops loose.

2. With two loops on the hook, rotate the hook counterclockwise by 360 degrees.

3. Wrap the yarn over the hook again and pull a loop through both loops on the hook. One twisted single crochet stitch made.

WORKING INTO ONE LOOP ONLY

If the hook is inserted under just one loop at the top of a stitch, the empty loop creates a ridge on either the front or the back of the fabric. "Front loop only" means the loop nearest to you, at the top of the stitch, and "back loop only" means the farther loop, whether you are working a right-side or a wrong-side row.

Front loop only (FLO)

If the hook is inserted under the front loop only, the empty back loop will show as a ridge on the other side of the work.

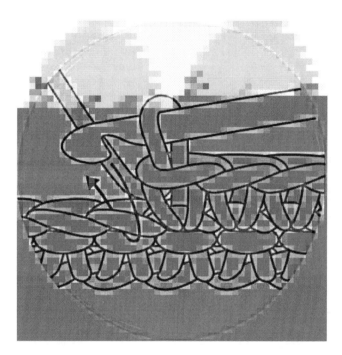

Back loop only (BLO)

If the hook is inserted under the back loop only, the empty front loop creates a ridge on the side of the work facing you. These examples show single crochet.

POST STITCHES

These are created by inserting the hook around the post of a stitch below—from the front or back—and are a great way to add texture to your crochet work. Front post stitches are slightly raised and back post stitches slightly recede. The two examples shown here are the front post double crochet (fpdc) and the back post double crochet (bpdc), which are the most common—but most regular stitches can be worked as front or back post stitches. The only thing that sets them apart is where they are worked.

Front post double crochet (fpdc)

1. Wrap the yarn over the hook. Inserting the hook through the work from front to back, take it from right to left around the post of the specified stitch below and then bring it through to the front again.

2. Wrap the yarn over the hook and pull through to make three loops on the hook. Wrap the yarn over again and pull through two loops on the hook. Wrap the yarn over once more and pull through both loops on the hook. So, you complete the stitch as you would a regular dc. A ridge forms on the other side of the work.

Back post double crochet (bpdc)

1. Wrap the yarn over the hook. Inserting the hook through the work from back to front, take it from right to left around the post of the specified stitch below and then take it through to the back again.

2. Complete as you would a regular dc, as explained in Step 2 of front post double crochet. A ridge forms on the side of the work facing you.

SPECIAL STITCHES

INCREASING AND DECREASING
Shaping in amigurumi is made by increasing (and decreasing) stitches, which means working two or more single crochet into the same stitch.

Working several stitches in the same place
This technique is used to increase the total number of stitches in a row or round. Increases may be worked at the edges of flat pieces, or at any point along a row. Two, three, or more stitches may be worked into the same place to make a fan of stitches, often called a shell.

Invisible decrease

Insert the hook into the front loop of the next two stitches and pull a loop through both. Wrap the yarn over the hook and pull through the last two loops on the hook.

POPCORN STITCH

A popcorn is a group of stitches worked in the same place and then folded and closed at the top so that the popcorn is raised from the background stitches. Work the specified number of stitches in the same place. Take the hook out of the working loop and insert it under both top loops of the first stitch of the popcorn. Pick up the working loop with the hook and draw it through to fold the group of stitches and close the popcorn at the top.

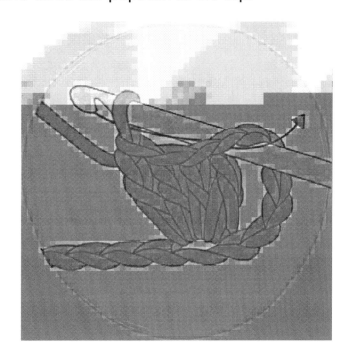

TECHNIQUES

CHANGING COLORS

Use this method for a neat join between colors. The first ball need not be fastened off; it may be left aside for a few rows or stitches in the course of a multicolored pattern.

1. Work up to the final "yarn over, pull through" of the last stitch in the old color and wrap the new color around the hook.

2. Use the new color to complete the stitch.

3. Continue in the new color.

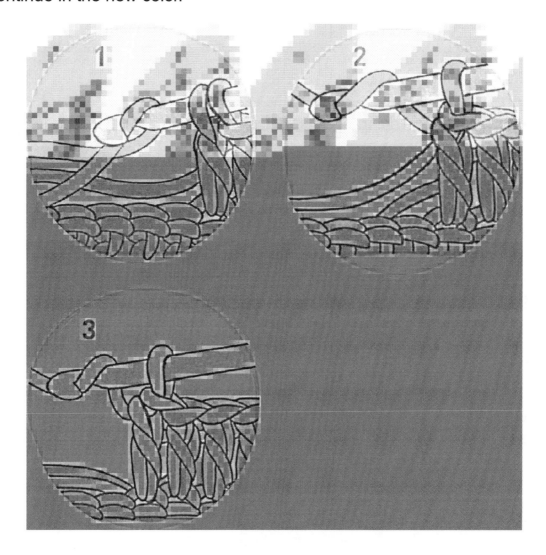

JOINING ROUNDS WITH A SLIP STITCH

Most amigurumi patterns are worked in continuous rounds without joins, but some pattern pieces require you to make a slip stitch join to the first stitch of the round, as shown.

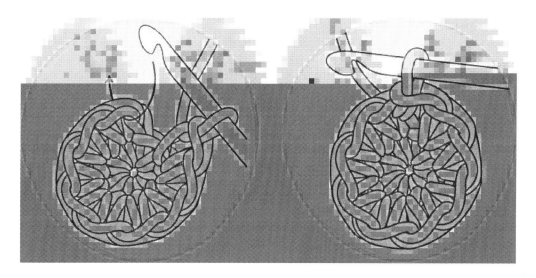

JOINING PARTS

Crochet pieces may be seamed with a tapestry needle. Use the same yarn as used for the main pieces, if possible. If this is too bulky, choose a matching, finer yarn, preferably with the same fiber content to avoid problems when the article is washed.

Backstitch seam

This is a firm seam that resists stretching. Hold the pieces with right sides together (pin them if necessary, as shown), matching the stitches or row ends, and use a tapestry needle and matching yarn to work backstitches, as shown.

Woven seam

This seam is flexible and flat. Lay the pieces with edges touching, wrong sides up, and use a tapestry needle and matching yarn to weave around the centers of the edge stitches, as shown. Do not pull the stitches too tightly; the seam should stretch as much as the work itself. When joining row ends, work in a similar way.

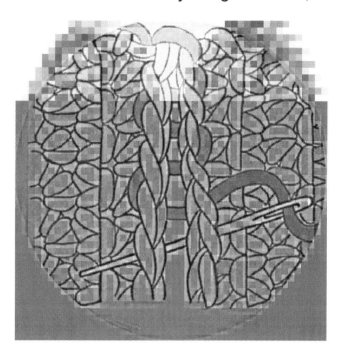

STUFFING

If you are using a loose filling such as polyester fiberfill, it is best to stuff as you go. This is easier than trying to poke the stuffing through a small opening at the end.

Take small amounts of stuffing and pull the fibers apart before placing in the doll. As more stuffing is placed inside, ensure that it reaches the edges and corners. You can prevent lumps by continuously filling rather than having breaks in the fiber.

If the stuffing becomes lumpy or starts clumping together, pull it out and start over. To ensure an even distribution, use the blunt end of a knitting needle or chopstick to move the stuffing around until you are happy.

EYES

Most of the dolls in the book have $^5/_{16}$" (8 mm) safety eyes—except for Bruce Lee, where $^5/_{16}$" (8 mm) oval safety eyes are used. However, If you make any of the dolls for children under the age of three, you might want to embroider the eyes for safety reasons. You can add them at the same stage that you embroider the eyebrows and nose.

If you are using safety eyes, cut two circles—a little larger than the safety eyes—from the white felt and make holes in the middle of the circles. Place the safety eyes into the holes. Insert them between rounds 17 and 18, with ten stitches between the eyes. Place the eyes on the opposite side to the start of the round.

EMBROIDERY

The facial features and other embroidered details are worked using backstitch. This stitch is useful for creating outlining and lines.

Bring the needle through from the back of the work. From the front and in one motion, take the needle through to the back a short distance along to the right, then draw it through the work to the front the same distance along to the left from the beginning of the stitch. Continue from right to left by inserting the needle through from front to back at the point where the last stitch emerged.

Made in United States
Orlando, FL
05 February 2024

43310609R00137